Teach Yourself
VISUALLY™
Macromedia® Dreamweaver® 8

Visual

by Janine Warner

WILEY

Wiley Publishing, Inc.

Teach Yourself VISUALLY™
Macromedia® Dreamweaver® 8

Published by
Wiley Publishing, Inc.
111 River Street
Hoboken, NJ 07030-5774

Published simultaneously in Canada

Library of Congress Control Number: 2005935144

ISBN-13: 978-0-7645-9998-9
ISBN-10: 0-7645-9998-4

Manufactured in the United States of America

10 9 8 7 6 5 4 3 2 1

Trademark Acknowledgments

Contact Us

For general information on our other products and services please contact our Customer Care Department within the U.S. at 800-762-2974, outside the U.S. at 317-572-3993 or fax 317-572-4002.

For technical support please visit www.wiley.com/techsupport.

Permissions

Avalon Houseboat

Black Heron Inn

Coastal Traveler

Inn on Tomales Bay

Kathryn LeMieux

Station House Café

Wiley Publishing, Inc.

Sales

Contact Wiley
at (800) 762-2974 or
fax (317) 572-4002.

Praise for Visual Books

"Like a lot of other people, I understand things best when I see them visually. Your books really make learning easy and life more fun."

John T. Frey (Cadillac, MI)

"I have quite a few of your Visual books and have been very pleased with all of them. I love the way the lessons are presented!"

Mary Jane Newman (Yorba Linda, CA)

"I just purchased my third Visual book (my first two are dog-eared now!), and, once again, your product has surpassed my expectations."

Tracey Moore (Memphis, TN)

"I am an avid fan of your Visual books. If I need to learn anything, I just buy one of your books and learn the topic in no time. Wonders! I have even trained my friends to give me Visual books as gifts."

Illona Bergstrom (Aventura, FL)

"Thank you for making it so clear. I appreciate it. I will buy many more Visual books."

J.P. Sangdong (North York, Ontario, Canada)

"I have several books from the Visual series and have always found them to be valuable resources."

Stephen P. Miller (Ballston Spa, NY)

"Thank you for the wonderful books you produce. It wasn't until I was an adult that I discovered how I learn – visually. Nothing compares to Visual books. I love the simple layout. I can just grab a book and use it at my computer, lesson by lesson. And I understand the material! You really know the way I think and learn. Thanks so much!"

Stacey Han (Avondale, AZ)

"I absolutely admire your company's work. Your books are terrific. The format is perfect, especially for visual learners like me. Keep them coming!"

Frederick A. Taylor, Jr. (New Port Richey, FL)

"I have several of your Visual books and they are the best I have ever used."

Stanley Clark (Crawfordville, FL)

"I bought my first Teach Yourself VISUALLY book last month. Wow. Now I want to learn everything in this easy format!"

Tom Vial (New York, NY)

"Thank you, thank you, thank you...for making it so easy for me to break into this high-tech world. I now own four of your books. I recommend them to anyone who is a beginner like myself."

Gay O'Donnell (Calgary, Alberta, Canada)

"I write to extend my thanks and appreciation for your books. They are clear, easy to follow, and straight to the point. Keep up the good work! I bought several of your books and they are just right! No regrets! I will always buy your books because they are the best."

Seward Kollie (Dakar, Senegal)

"Compliments to the chef!! Your books are extraordinary! Or, simply put, extra-ordinary, meaning way above the rest! THANK YOU THANK YOU THANK YOU! I buy them for friends, family, and colleagues."

Christine J. Manfrin (Castle Rock, CO)

"What fantastic teaching books you have produced! Congratulations to you and your staff. You deserve the Nobel Prize in Education in the Software category. Thanks for helping me understand computers."

Bruno Tonon (Melbourne, Australia)

"Over time, I have bought a number of your 'Read Less - Learn More' books. For me, they are THE way to learn anything easily. I learn easiest using your method of teaching."

José A. Mazón (Cuba, NY)

"I am an avid purchaser and reader of the Visual series, and they are the greatest computer books I've seen. The Visual books are perfect for people like myself who enjoy the computer, but want to know how to use it more efficiently. Your books have definitely given me a greater understanding of my computer, and have taught me to use it more effectively. Thank you very much for the hard work, effort, and dedication that you put into this series."

Alex Diaz (Las Vegas, NV)

Credits

Acquisitions Editor
Jody Lefevere

Product Development Manager
Lindsay Sandman

Copy Editor
Marylouise Wiack

Technical Editor
David LaFontaine

Editorial Manager
Robyn Siesky

Permissions Editor
Laura Moss

Manufacturing
Allan Conley
Linda Cook
Paul Gilchrist
Jennifer Guynn

Illustrators
Steven Amory
Matthew Bell
Ronda David-Burroughs
Cheryl Grubbs
Jacob Mansfield
Rita Marley
Kristin Corley
Paul Schmitt

Book Design
Kathie Rickard

Production Coordinator
Adrienne Martinez

Layout
Jennifer Heleine
Amanda Spagnuolo

Screen Artist
Jill A. Proll

Proofreader
Shannon Ramsey

Quality Control
Brian H. Walls

Indexer
Stephen Ingle

Special Help
Macromedia, Inc.

Vice President and Executive Group Publisher
Richard Swadley

Vice President and Publisher
Barry Pruett

Composition Director
Debbie Stailey

About the Author

Janine Warner is a best-selling author, journalist, and Internet consultant. Since 1995, she's written and coauthored 10 books about the Internet, including *Creating Family Web Sites For Dummies* and *Dreamweaver 8 For Dummies*.

A recognized Internet expert known for making technology fun and accessible, Janine has been a featured guest on technology news specials on ABC, NBC and ZDTV and has been interviewed on numerous radio programs in the United States and abroad. Her articles and columns have been published in a variety of publications, including *The Miami Herald* newspaper, *Shape Magazine*, and the Pulitzer Prize Winning *Point Reyes Light*.

Janine is a popular speaker at conferences and events throughout the US, and her fluency in Spanish has brought her many invitations to speak in Latin America and Spain. She also serves as a judge for the Arroba de Oro, a series of Internet award contests held throughout Latin America. Through her participation as a speaker at the award's events, she helped to create an Internet literacy program for high school students in Central America.

Janine has served as a part-time faculty member at the University of Southern California Annenberg School for Communication and the University of Miami. She now serves as the Multimedia Program Manager for the Western Knight Center, a joint project of USC and UC Berkeley, funded by the Knight Foundation.

From 1998 to 2000, Janine worked fulltime for *The Miami Herald*, first as their Online Managing Editor and later as Director of New Media, managing a team of designers, programmers, and journalists who produced the online editions of *The Miami Herald* and *El Nuevo Herald*, as well as Miami.com. She also served as Director of Latin American Operations for CNET Networks, an international technology media company.

An award-winning former reporter, she earned a degree in Journalism and Spanish from the University of Massachusetts, Amherst, and worked for several years in Northern California as a reporter and editor before becoming interested in the Internet in the mid-'90s. To learn more, visit www.JCWarner.com

Author's Acknowledgments

I used to try and thank many people in my books — former teachers, mentors, friends — but I have been graced by so many wonderful people now that no publisher will give me enough pages to thank them all. So I focus here on the people who made *this* book possible.

First, let me thank Frank Vera, a great programmer who helped with the most technical aspects of the last chapter of this book. Thanks also to Sheila Castelli, who designed many of the Web sites featured in the examples in this book. You can find her work online at www.digitalcottage.com. Thanks to the project editor for her attention to detail and helping make sure all the final pieces came together in this book. Thanks also to Jody Lefevere for taking this project through the development process. Thanks to my brother Kevin, his lovely wife Stephanie, and their three adorable children, Mikayla, Savannah, and Jessica whose photos illustrate my Digital Family Web site, which is featured in some of the exercises in this book and can be found online at www.digitalfamily.com.

I've written acknowledgements for so many books now I think my parents have lost count, but I always send them copies and I always thank them. I love you all — Malinda, Janice, Helen, and Robin. Thank you for your love, support, and understanding.

Table of Contents

chapter 3   Exploring the Dreamweaver Interface

chapter 4   Working with HTML

Table of Contents

chapter 7 Creating Hyperlinks

chapter 8 Using Tables to Design a Web Page

Table of Contents

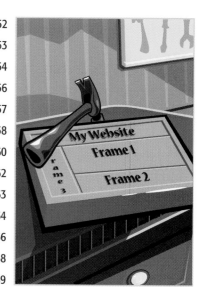

chapter 11

Using Library Items and Templates

chapter 12

Creating and Applying Cascading Style Sheets

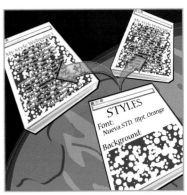

Table of Contents

chapter 13   Using Layers to Increase User Interaction

chapter 14   Publishing a Web Site

How to Use This Book

Do you look at the pictures in a book or newspaper before anything else on a page? Would you rather see an image instead of read about how to do something? Search no further. This book is for you. Opening *Teach Yourself VISUALLY Macromedia Dreamweaver 8* allows you to read less and learn more about Dreamweaver.

Who Needs This Book

This book is for a reader who has never used this particular technology or software application. It is also for more computer literate individuals who want to expand their knowledge of the different features that Dreamweaver 8 has to offer.

Book Organization

Teach Yourself VISUALLY Macromedia Dreamweaver 8 has 16 chapters. Each chapter is divided into task sections.

Chapter Organization

This book consists of sections, all listed in the book's table of contents. A *section* is a set of steps that show you how to complete a specific computer task.

Each section, usually contained on two facing pages, has an introduction to the task at hand, a set of full-color screen shots and steps that walk you through the task, and a set of tips. This format allows you to quickly look at a topic of interest and learn it instantly.

Chapters group together three or more sections with a common theme. A chapter may also contain pages that give you the background information needed to understand the sections in a chapter.

Chapter 1 introduces you to the World Wide Web, the different types of information you can put on a Web site, and shows you how to start Dreamweaver.

Chapter 2 illustrates how to set up your Web site. You will learn how to start a project in Dreamweaver by setting up a local site on your computer and then creating the first Web page of the site.

Chapter 3 takes you on a tour of the panels and windows that make up the Dreamweaver interface. You will discover all of the handy tools and features that make this an award-winning Web design program.

Chapter 4 introduces the code behind your pages and the tools in Dreamweaver that enable you to edit HTML code. Dreamweaver helps you to build Web pages by automatically writing the HTML code as you create pages in the design area.

Chapter 5 walks you through formatting and styling text, for example, creating headlines, paragraphs, bulleted lists, and stylized text. Text is the easiest type of information to add to a Web page using Dreamweaver.

Chapter 6 shows you how to insert and format these elements. You can make your Web page much more interesting by adding digital photos, scanned art, animation, and interactive visual elements.

Chapter 7 illustrates how to use both text and images as hyperlinks to connect related information. Using Dreamweaver, you can create links from one page to another in your Web site, or to other Web sites on the Internet. You will also learn how to create e-mail links and image maps.

Chapter 8 walks you through creating and formatting tables. Tables enable you to arrange text, images, and other elements on your Web pages, and to create complex designs, even within the constraints of HTML.

Chapter 9 demonstrates how to divide the display area of a Web browser into multiple panes by creating frames. Frames offer another way to organize information by splitting up your pages. For example, you can keep linked content visible in one frame and target it to open in a different frame within the same browser window.

Chapter 10 helps you to create forms on your Web pages that will enable your Web site visitors to send you information. You will discover how to create forms with different types of fields, buttons, and menus.

Chapter 11 takes you through the process of using library items and templates to quickly create consistent page designs. You can save time by storing frequently used Web page elements and layouts as library items, and saving complete page designs as templates.

Chapter 12 illustrates how to use Cascading Style Sheets to create and apply formatting. Cascading Style Sheets can save you a lot of tedious formatting time, especially on big Web sites.

Chapter 13 shows you how to gain more design control and increase user interaction using the Layers feature. In addition to other layout tools, Dreamweaver allows you to quickly create layers.

Chapter 14 walks you through the process of publishing your Web site, and keeping it up-to-date with Dreamweaver. You can publish your completed Web pages on a server to allow the world to view them.

Chapter 15 details how to maintain a Web site. Maintaining a Web site and keeping its content fresh can be as much work as creating the site. Dreamweaver's site-maintenance tools make updating faster and easier.

Chapter 16 is an advanced chapter on building a database-driven Web site. If you are an advanced Dreamweaver user who understands databases, then you can read this chapter to learn how to use server behaviors to create powerful and dynamic Web sites.

What You Need to Use This Book

The minimum requirements for performing the tasks in this book are as follows.

Windows Users

- Windows 2000 or Windows XP
- Intel Pentium III processor (or equivalent) and later running at 800 MHz
- 256 MB RAM installed on your computer; for best performance, 1 GB recommended to run more than one Studio 8 product simultaneously
- 1024 x 768, 16-bit display (32-bit recommended)
- 650 MB available disk space

Macintosh Users

- Mac OS X 10.3, 10.4
- 600 MHz PowerPC G3 and later
- 256 MB RAM installed on your computer; for best performance, 1 GB recommended to run more than one Studio 8 product simultaneously
- 1024 x 768, thousands of colors display (millions of colors recommended)
- 300 MB available disk space

Using the Mouse

This book uses the following conventions to describe the actions you perform when using the mouse:

Click

Press your left mouse button once. You generally position and click your mouse to select something on the screen.

Double-click

Press your left mouse button twice. Double-clicking something on the computer screen generally opens whatever item you have double-clicked.

Right-click

Press your right mouse button. When you right-click anything on the computer screen, the program displays a shortcut menu containing commands specific to the selected item.

Click and Drag, and Release the Mouse

Move your mouse pointer and hover it over an item on the screen. Press and hold down the left mouse button. Now, move the mouse to where you want to place the item and then release the button. You use this method to move an item from one area of the computer screen to another.

The Conventions in This Book

A number of typographic and layout styles have been used throughout *Teach Yourself VISUALLY Macromedia Dreamweaver 8* to distinguish different types of information.

Bold

Bold type represents the names of commands and options that you interact with. Bold type also indicates text and numbers that you must type into a dialog box or window.

Italics

Italic words introduce a new term and are followed by a definition.

Numbered Steps

You must perform the instructions in numbered steps in order to successfully complete a section and achieve the final results.

Bulleted Steps

These steps point out various optional features. You do not have to perform these steps; they simply give additional information about a feature.

Indented Text

Indented text tells you what the program does in response to you following a numbered step. For example, if you click a certain menu command, a dialog box may appear, or a window may open. Indented text may also tell you what the final result is when you follow a set of numbered steps.

Notes

Notes give additional information. They may describe special conditions that may occur during an operation. They may warn you of a situation that you want to avoid, for example the loss of data. A note may also cross reference a related area of the book. A cross reference may guide you to another chapter, or another section with the current chapter.

Icons and buttons

Icons and buttons are graphical representations within the text. They show you exactly what you need to click to perform a step.

 You can easily identify the tips in any section by looking for the TIPS icon. Tips offer additional information, including tips, hints, and tricks. You can use the TIPS information to go beyond what you have learned in the steps.

Operating System Difference

The program is designed to work the same on both platforms, with the exception of minor interface differences, it is the same.

Getting Started
with Dreamweaver

This chapter describes
the World Wide Web,
introduces the
different types of
information you can
put on a Web site,
and shows you how
to start Dreamweaver.

Introduction to the World Wide Web

You can use Dreamweaver to create and publish pages on the World Wide Web.

World Wide Web

The *World Wide Web* (Web) is a global collection of documents located on Internet-connected computers. You can access the Web by using a Web browser. Web pages are connected to one another by hyperlinks that you can click.

Web Site

A *Web site* is a collection of linked Web pages stored on a Web server. Most Web sites have a *home page* that describes the information located on the Web site and provides a place where people can start their exploration of the Web site. The pages of a good Web site are intuitively organized and have a common theme.

Dreamweaver

Dreamweaver is a program that enables you to create Web pages with hyperlinks, text, images, and multimedia. You can create your Web pages on your computer and then use Dreamweaver to transfer the finished files to a Web server where others can view them on the Web.

HTML

Hypertext Markup Language (HTML) is the formatting language used to create Web pages. You can use Dreamweaver to create Web pages without knowing HTML because Dreamweaver writes the HTML for you behind the scenes.

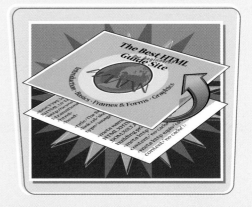

Web Server

A *Web server* is a computer that is connected to the Internet and has software that serves Web pages to visitors. Each Web page that you view in a Web browser on the World Wide Web resides on a Web server somewhere on the Internet. When you are ready to publish your pages on the Web, you can use Dreamweaver to transfer your files to a Web server.

Web Browser

A *Web browser* is a program that can download Web documents from the Internet, interpret HTML, and then display the Web page text and any associated images and multimedia. Two popular Web browsers are Microsoft Internet Explorer and Netscape Navigator.

Parts of a Web Page

You can communicate your message on the Web in a variety of ways. The following are some of the common elements that appear on Web pages.

Text

Text is the simplest type of content that you can publish on the Web. Dreamweaver enables you to change the size, color, and font of the text on your Web page and to organize it into paragraphs, headings, and lists. Perhaps the best thing about text is that practically everyone can view it, no matter what type of Web browser or Internet connection a person may have, and it downloads very quickly.

Images

For your Web site, you can take photos with a digital camera, and you can scan drawings, logos, or other images for the Web by using a scanner. You can also create and edit images in a graphics program, such as Adobe Photoshop or Macromedia Fireworks, and then place them on Web pages with Dreamweaver.

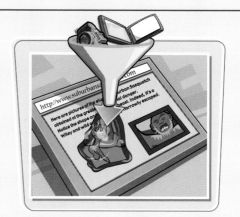

Hyperlinks

Usually called a *link*, a *hyperlink* is text or an image that has been associated with another file. You can open the other file in a Web browser by clicking the hyperlink. Although hyperlinks usually link to other Web pages or other Web sites, they can also link to other locations on the same page or to other types of files.

Tables

Although tables organize information in columns and rows on your Web page, you can use them for much more than just organizing data. Tables provide one of the best ways to create complex Web designs. By turning off the borders of a table and setting it to span an entire page, you can use the table to organize the entire layout of the page. See Chapter 9 for more information about tables.

Forms

Forms reverse the information flow on Web sites, thus enabling visitors to your Web site to send information back to you. With Dreamweaver, you can create forms that include text fields, drop-down menus, radio buttons, and other elements.

Frames

In a framed Web site, the Web browser window is divided into several rectangular frames, and a different Web page loads into each frame. Users can scroll through content in each frame, independently of the content in the other frames. Dreamweaver offers visual tools for building frame-based Web sites.

Plan Your Web Site

Carefully planning your pages before you build them can help to ensure that your finished Web site looks great and is well organized. Before you start building your Web site, take a little time to organize your ideas and gather the materials that you will need.

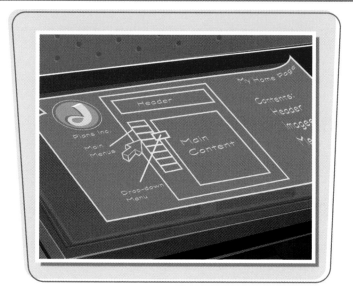

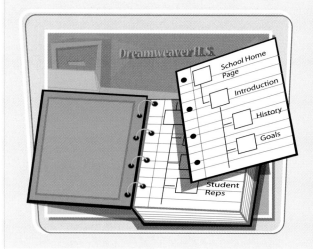

Organize Your Ideas

Build your Web site on paper before you start building it in Dreamweaver. Sketching out a Web site map, with rectangles representing Web pages and arrows representing links, can help you to visualize the size and scope of your project. Use sticky notes if you want to move pages around as you plan your Web site.

Gather Your Content

Before you start building your Web site, gather all of the elements that you want to use. This process may require writing text, taking photos, and designing graphics. It can also involve producing multimedia content, such as audio and video files. Gathering all of your material together in the beginning makes it easier for you to organize your Web site once you start building it in Dreamweaver.

Define Your Audience

Identifying your target audience can help you to decide what kind of content to offer on your Web site. For example, you may create a very different design for small children than for adults. It is important to know whether visitors are using the latest Web browser technology and how fast they can view advanced features, such as multimedia.

Host Your Finished Web Site

To make your finished Web site accessible on the Web, you need to store, or *host*, it on a Web server. Most people have their Web sites hosted on a Web server at a commercial Internet service provider (ISP) or at their company or university.

You can start Dreamweaver on a PC
and begin building pages that you can
publish on the Web. You first need to
purchase and install Dreamweaver if
you do not have it already.

Starting ...

Start Dreamweaver on a PC

1 Click **Start**.

2 Click **All Programs**.

3 Click **Macromedia**.

4 Click **Macromedia Dreamweaver 8**.

*Note: Your path to the Dreamweaver application may be different,
depending on how you installed your software and your operating system.*

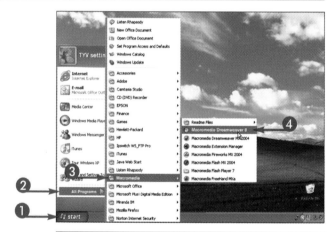

The Dreamweaver Start screen appears.

Start Dreamweaver on a Macintosh

You can start Dreamweaver on a Macintosh and begin building pages that you can publish on the Web. You first need to purchase and install Dreamweaver if you do not have it already.

Start Dreamweaver on a Macintosh

① Double-click your hard drive.

② Double-click the **Macromedia Dreamweaver 8** folder (📁).

③ Double-click the **Dreamweaver 8** icon (🔵).

Note: *The exact location of the Dreamweaver folder depends on how you installed your software.*

The Dreamweaver Start screen appears.

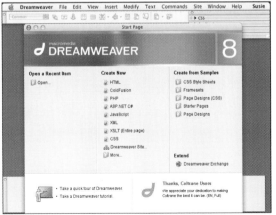

Tour the Dreamweaver Interface on a PC

Dreamweaver 8 on a PC features a variety of windows, panels, and inspectors.

Toolbar
Contains shortcuts to preview and display features, and a text field where you can specify the title of a page.

Properties Inspector
Used to display and edit attributes of any element selected in the Document window.

Panels
Windows that provide access to the Design, Code, Application, Tag, Files, Layers, and History panels.

Document Window
The main workspace where you insert and arrange the text, images, and other elements of your Web page.

Menus
Contain the commands for using Dreamweaver. Many of these commands are duplicated within the windows, panels, and inspectors of Dreamweaver.

Insert Bar
Used to implement page elements and technology. There are several different Insert bars that you can select, depending on the type of element you want to insert in your page.

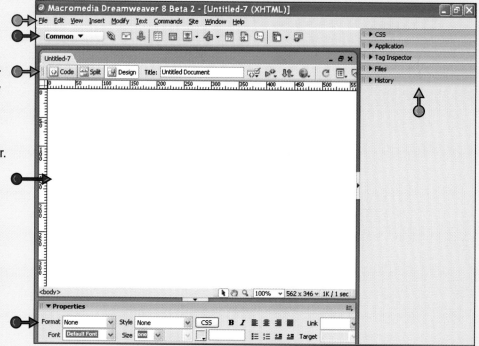

Dreamweaver 8 on a Macintosh features a variety of windows, panels, and inspectors.

Document Window

The main workspace where you insert and arrange the text, images, and other elements of your Web page.

Panels

Windows that provide access to the Design, Code, Application, Files, Advanced Layout, Answers, and History panels.

Properties Inspector

Used to display and edit attributes of any element selected in the Document window.

Toolbar

Contains shortcuts to preview and display features, and a text field where you can specify the title of a page.

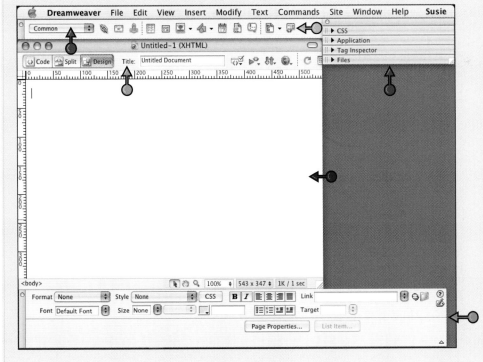

Menus

Contain the commands for using Dreamweaver. Many of these commands are duplicated within the windows, panels, and inspectors of Dreamweaver.

Insert Bar

Used to implement page elements and technology. There are several different Insert bars that you can select, depending on the type of element you want to insert in your page.

You can show or hide accessory windows, also called panels and inspectors, by using commands in the Window menu.

Show or Hide a Window

1 Click **Window**.

2 Click the window that you want to open.

This example opens the Properties window.

● A ☑ next to a window name indicates that the window is open.

● Dreamweaver displays the window.

To hide a window, click **Window** and then click the check-marked (☑) window name.

You can click **Window** and then click **Hide Panels** to hide everything except the Document window and toolbar.

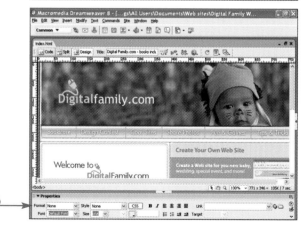

Exit Dreamweaver

You can exit Dreamweaver to close the program.

You should always exit Dreamweaver and all other programs before turning off your computer.

Exit Dreamweaver

① Click **File**.

② Click **Exit (Quit)**.

● Before closing, Dreamweaver alerts you to save any open documents that have unsaved changes.

③ Click **Yes**.

Dreamweaver exits.

You can use the help tools that are built into Dreamweaver to get answers to your questions or to learn techniques that you do not know.

Get Help

① Click **Help**.

② Click **Dreamweaver Help**.

You can also click the **Help** icon (⊙) in the Properties inspector.

The Using Dreamweaver help page opens.

● You can click the **Contents** tab to scroll and select available Help topics.

● You can click the **Index** tab to access a list of topics.

③ Click the **Search** tab to search for a specific topic.

The Search window appears.

④ Type one or more keywords, separating multiple keywords with a plus sign (+) for your search.

⑤ Click **List Topics**.

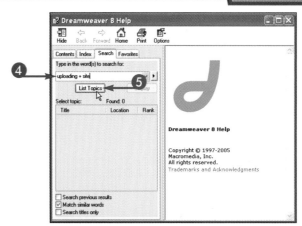

A list of topics appears.

⑥ Click a topic from the search result list.

⑦ Click **Display**.

● Information appears on your topic.

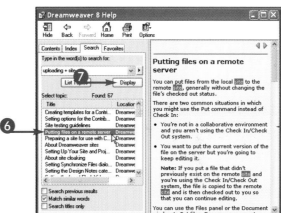

TIP

Are there different ways of opening the Help tools and other options in Dreamweaver?

Very often, yes. For example, you may be able to access a command, such as Modify Page Properties, by using either a menu or the Properties inspector. You can also use the Split or Code options to view and edit the HTML code directly, if you know how to write HTML.

Setting Up Your Web Site

You start a project in Dreamweaver by setting up a local site on your computer and then creating the first Web page of the site. This chapter shows you how to set up your Web site.

Set Up a New Web Site

Before you create your Web pages, you need to define your site in Dreamweaver. You must create a folder on your local hard drive where you can store your HTML, images, and other files. Defining a local site enables you to manage your Web page files in the Site window. For more information on the Site window, see Chapter 14.

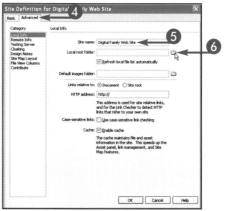

Set Up a Web Site

① Click the **Manage Sites** link in the Files panel.

The Manage Sites dialog box appears.

② Click **New**.

③ Click **Site**.

The Site Definition dialog box appears.

④ Click the **Advanced** tab.

⑤ Type a name for your site.

⑥ Click the Folder icon (📁) to search for your Web site folder.

The Choose local root folder dialog box appears.

7 Click here and select the folder that stores your Web pages.

● You can create a new folder by clicking and then selecting that folder.

8 Click **Select**.

9 Click and select the folder where you want to store the images for your Web site.

10 Type the URL (Web address or domain name) of your Web site.

11 Click this option to enable the cache, which makes it faster to create links (changes to).

12 Click **OK**.

13 In the Manage Sites Window, click **Done**.

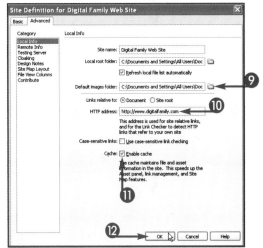

TIP

Why is it important to keep all of my Web site files in a main folder on my computer?

Keeping everything in the same folder enables you to easily transfer your Web site files to a Web server without changing the organization of the files. If you do not organize your Web site files on the Web server in the same way they are organized on your local computer, then hyperlinks may not work, and images may not display properly. For more information about working with Web site files, see Chapter 14.

Create a New Web Page

A new feature in Dreamweaver 8 is the initial Start Page. There are many useful shortcuts on this page, including some for creating a new Web page.

Create a New Web Page

① Click **File**.

② Click **New.**

The New Document dialog box appears.

③ Click **Basic page**.

④ Click **HTML**.

⑤ Click **Create**.

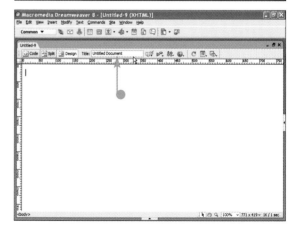

● An Untitled Document window appears.

Note: The page name and filename are untitled until you save them.

You can also create preformatted pages by choosing the Page Designs category in the New Document dialog box.

A Web page title appears in the title bar when the page opens in a Web browser. The title helps search engines to index pages with more accuracy, and is saved in a user's Bookmark list if they bookmark your Web page.

Add a Title to a Web Page

1 Type a name for your Web page in the Title text box.

2 Press `Enter` (`Return`).

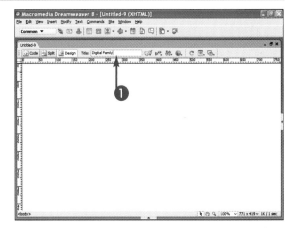

● The Web page title appears in the title bar when the page displays in a Web browser.

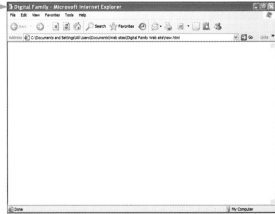

Save a Web Page

You should save your Web page before closing the program or transferring the page to a remote site. It is also a good idea to save all of your files frequently to prevent work from being lost due to power outages or system failures. For more information about connecting to remote sites, see Chapter 14.

Save a Web Page

SAVE YOUR DOCUMENT

1. Click **File**.

2. Click **Save**.

● You can click **Save As** to save an existing file with a new filename.

If you are saving a new file for the first time, then the Save As dialog box appears.

3. Click here and select your local site folder.

4. Type a name for your Web page.

Your local site folder is where you want to save the pages and other files for your Web site.

5. Click **Save**.

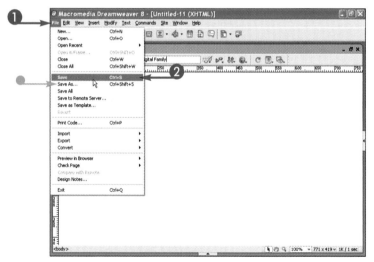

● Dreamweaver saves the Web page, and the filename and path appear in the title bar.

● You can click ✕ to close the page.

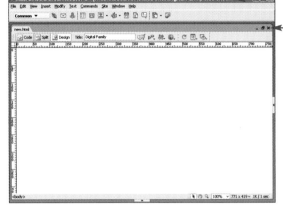

REVERT A PAGE

1 Click **File**.

2 Click **Revert**.

The page reverts to the previously saved version. All of the changes made since the last time you saved the file are lost.

Note: If you exit Dreamweaver after you save a document, Dreamweaver cannot revert to the previous version.

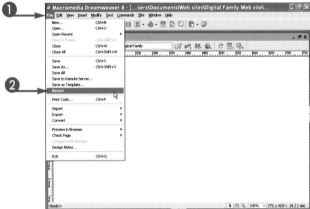

TIP

Why should I name the main page of my site index.html?

You should name your main Web site or home page index.html because that is the filename that most Web servers open first when a user types a domain name into a Web browser. If you name your main page index.html and it does not open as your first page when your site is on the server, then check with your system administrator or hosting service.

Preview a Web Page in a Browser

You can see how your Web page will appear online by previewing it in a Web browser. The Preview in Browser command works with any Web browser that is installed on your computer. Although Dreamweaver does not ship with Web browser software, Internet Explorer is preinstalled on most computers.

① Click **Preview in Browser** ().

② Click a Web browser from the drop-down menu that appears.

You can also preview the page in your primary Web browser by pressing F12 .

Your Web browser launches and opens the current page.

The file has a temporary filename for viewing in the Web browser.

ADD/REMOVE BROWSER

1. Click **File**.

2. Click **Preview In Browser**.

3. Click **Edit Browser List**.

The Preferences dialog box appears.

4. Click ⊞ to open the Add Browser dialog box.

5. Type a name for your Web browser.

6. Click **Browse** and select a Web browser for your computer.

7. Click **OK** to close the Add Browser dialog box.

8. Click **OK** to close the Preferences dialog box.

The newly added Web browser appears in the browser list.

Why can I use more than one Web browser for previews?
Dreamweaver allows you to add more than one Web browser because not all Web browsers display Web pages the same way; for example, Lynx is a text-based Web browser. By using the browser list, you can easily test your Web page in a different Web browser with just a few mouse-clicks.

3

Exploring the Dreamweaver Interface

Take a tour of the panels and windows that make up the Dreamweaver interface. You will discover all of the handy tools and features that make this an award-winning Web design program.

Customize the Document Window

The Document window is the main workspace in Dreamweaver, where you create Web pages and enter and format text, images, and other elements. You can open and close the customizable panels to keep the workspace clear when you are not using them.

Customize the Document Window

- You can use the drop-down menu to change the options in the Insert bar.
- The status bar displays the file size and estimated download time for the page.

① Click ▯ on the panels that you want to close.

The panels close.

- You can click ▯ again to bring the panels back.

② Click the **Properties** ▽.

● The Properties inspector expands to reveal additional options for any selected image or element.

③ Click **Split view** ( ).

The Document window splits to display both the Code and Design views.

● When you select an element in one view, it is highlighted in the other view, thus making it easy to find formatting tags.

● You can hide the Code view by clicking **Design view** ( ).

● You can click **Code view** ( ) to view just the HTML code.

TIP

How can I keep my favorite features handy?

You can open or close any of the panels and inspectors in Dreamweaver so that your favorite features are handy when you need them and others are out of the way when you do not need them. Most of the panels and other options are available from the Windows menu. For example, to open the History panel, click **Window** and then click **History**. As you work, you may choose to have different panels opened or closed to give you more workspace or provide easier access to the features you are using.

Format Content with the Properties Inspector

The Properties inspector enables you to view the properties associated with the object or text that is currently selected in the Document window. Text fields, drop-down menus, buttons, and other form elements in the Properties inspector allow you to modify these properties.

FORMAT AN IMAGE

① Click to select an image.

● The image properties appear.

You can change many image properties in the Properties inspector, such as dimensions, filename, and alignment.

② Click the **Align** ▾.

③ To wrap the text around the image, click to select an alignment.

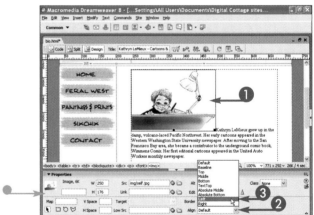

● The text automatically wraps around the image when you apply Left alignment.

④ Click and drag to select text.

● The text properties appear.

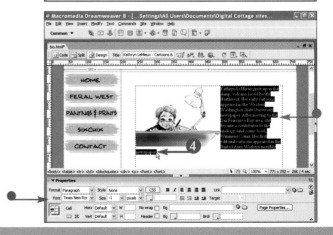

FORMAT TEXT

⑤ With the text selected, click the **Font** ▾.

⑥ Click the **Arial, Helvetica, sans-serif** font.

This font selection is easy to read on a computer screen.

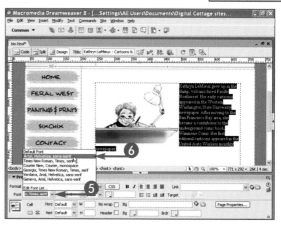

● Your text automatically changes to reflect your formatting choices in the Properties inspector.

You can change many text properties in the Properties inspector, such as format, size, and alignment.

● You can click the **Properties arrow** to switch between standard and expanded modes for the inspector.

 TIP

When would I use more than one font on a Web page?
When you choose a font face in Dreamweaver, the program offers fonts in groups of three. For example, one option is Arial, Helvetica, and sans-serif, and another option is Times New Roman, Times, and serif. Dreamweaver provides these collections because the fonts that display on a Web page are determined by the available fonts on the visitor's computer. Because you cannot guarantee what fonts a user will have, Web browsers use the first font that matches in a list of fonts. Thus, in the first example, the font will display in Arial if it is on the visitor's computer, or in Helvetica if Arial is not available, or in any available sans-serif font if neither of the first two fonts is available.

Add an E-Mail Link from the Insert Panel

You can insert elements, such as images, tables, and layers, into your pages with the Insert panel. Located at the top of the window, the panel features a drop-down menu that reveals options such as Common elements, Forms, and Text.

① Click here and select **Common**.

② Click and drag to select text.

③ Click **Email Link** (📧).

The Email Link dialog box appears.

④ Type an e-mail address.

⑤ Click **OK**.

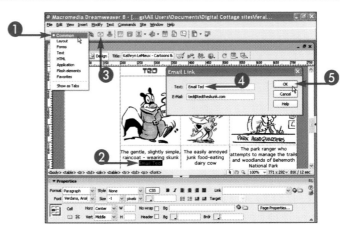

● In this example, the text changes into an e-mail hyperlink.

You can click any button in the Insert panel to add that element to your document.

The History panel keeps track of the commands that you perform in Dreamweaver. When you backtrack through those commands, you can return your page to a previous state. This is a convenient way to correct errors.

Correct Errors with the History Panel

① Click **Window**.

② Click **History**.

● The History panel appears.

● To undo one or more commands, click and drag the slider (▣) upward.

To redo the commands, click and drag the ▣ downward.

Note: *If you scroll backward, the later changes are deleted. You can only add steps to the end of the sequence.*

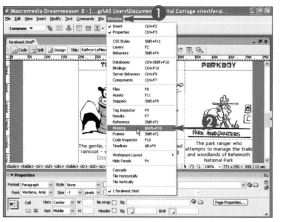

Dreamweaver 8 features an uncluttered workspace with windows that lock into place and panels that you can expand or collapse. You can also rearrange panels and move them around the screen to customize the interface.

❶ Click **Window**.

❷ Click **Files**.

● The Files panel appears and displays all of the files in the Web site.

❸ Click the **Assets** tab.

The Assets panel appears.

❹ Click **Images** (▦).

● All of the available images in the site appear in the Assets panel.

⑤ Click any image filename to preview the image in the display area at the top of the Assets panel.

⑥ Click the **Files** tab to collapse the panel.

● The Assets panel collapses.

Note: When you collapse a panel, such as the Files panel, other panels become more visible.

● You can click ▶ to expand any panel.

How can I keep track of my assets?

The Assets panel provides access to many handy features, such as the Colors assets, which list all of the colors that are used on a site. For example, this is useful if you are using a particular text color and you want to use the same color consistently on every page. Similarly, the Links assets make it easy to access links that are used elsewhere in your site so that you can quickly and easily set frequently used links.

Create and Apply a Custom Command

You can select a sequence of commands that have been recorded in the History panel, and save the sequence as a custom command. The new command appears under the Commands menu. You can apply it to other elements on the page to automate repetitive tasks.

① Select an element and perform a sequence of commands.

In this example, text is formatted in bold and italics.

If the History panel is not open, click **Window** and then click **History**.

② To select the steps that you want to save as a single command, Ctrl +click (Shift +click) each selection.

③ Right-click the selection.

④ Click **Save As Command** from the drop-down menu that appears.

The Save As Command dialog box appears.

⑤ Type a name for the command.

⑥ Click **OK**.

Dreamweaver saves the command.

Note: You cannot use this feature with all commands. For example, clicking and dragging an element cannot be included in a command.

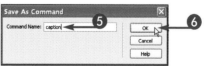

APPLY THE COMMAND

1 Select the element to which you want to apply the command.

2 Click **Commands**.

3 Click the command that you want to apply.

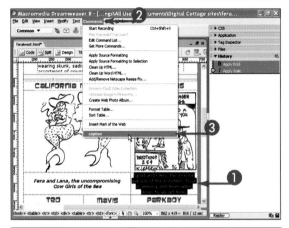

● Dreamweaver applies the command to the selection.

TIP

How do I change the name of a custom command?

1 Click **Commands**.

2 Click **Edit Command List**.

The Edit Command List dialog box appears, listing the custom commands.

3 Click a command, and then type a new name.

4 Click **Close**.

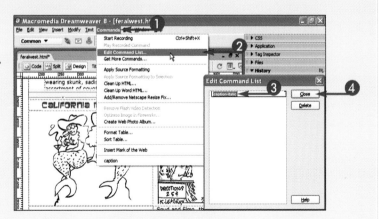

Set
Preferences

You can easily change the default appearance and behavior of Dreamweaver by specifying settings in the Preferences dialog box. You can modify the user interface of Dreamweaver to better suit how you like to work.

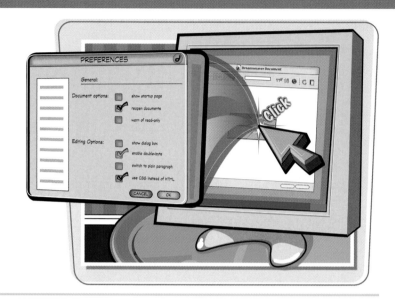

Set Preferences

① Click **Edit**.

② Click **Preferences**.

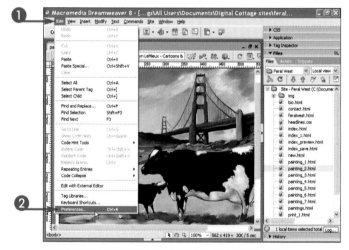

The Preferences dialog box appears.

③ Click a Preferences category.

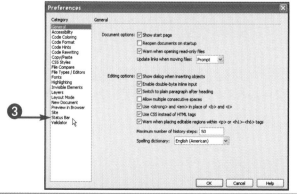

● Options appear for the category you selected.

④ Click here and select a new option.

● In this example, the Connection Speed option is set to 128K.

⑤ Click **OK**.

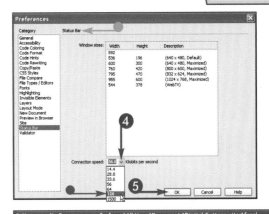

● The preference changes take effect immediately.

In this example, the status bar now displays download times that assume a 128K connection speed.

TIP

How do I ensure that Dreamweaver does not change my HTML or other code?

You can select options under the Code Rewriting category in the Preferences dialog box to ensure that Dreamweaver does not automatically correct or modify your code. For example, you can turn off the error-correcting functions, specify the files that it should not rewrite based on file extension, or disable the character encoding features.

Working with HTML

Dreamweaver helps you to build Web pages by automatically writing the HTML code as you create pages in the design area. This chapter introduces the code behind your pages and the tools in Dreamweaver that enable you to edit HTML code.

Although Dreamweaver writes the HTML code for you and saves you time, you always have the option of writing or editing the code yourself.

HTML

Hypertext Markup Language (HTML) is the formatting language that you can use to create Web pages. When you open a Web page in a Web browser, the HTML code tells the Web browser how to display the text, images, and other content on the page. Although it can do many other things, at its most basic level, Dreamweaver is an HTML-writing application.

HTML Tags

The basic unit of HTML is called a *tag*. You can recognize HTML tags by their angle brackets:

```
<p>Today the weather is
<b>nice</b>.<br>Tomorrow it may
<i>rain</i>.</p>
```

You can format text and other elements on your page by placing them inside the HTML tags.

How Tags Work

Some HTML tags work in pairs; opening and closing tags surround content in a document and control the formatting of the content. For example: <b> tags set off bold text; closing tags are documented by a forward slash (/); other tags can stand alone, such as the <br> tag that adds a line break. HTML tags are not case-sensitive; you can use uppercase, lowercase, or mixed-case letters.

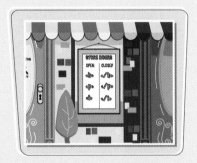

Create Web Pages without Knowing HTML

Dreamweaver streamlines the process of creating Web pages by giving you an easy-to-use, visual interface with which to generate HTML code. You specify formatting with menu commands and button clicks, and Dreamweaver takes care of writing the underlying HTML code. When you build a Web page in the Document window, you can see your page as it will appear in a Web browser, instead of as HTML code.

HTML Documents

Because HTML documents are plain text files, you can open and edit them with any text editor. In fact, in the early days of the Web, most people created their pages with simple editors such as Notepad (in Windows) and SimpleText (in Macintosh). However, writing HTML manually is a slow, tedious process, especially when creating advanced HTML elements such as tables, forms, and frames.

Direct Access to the HTML

Dreamweaver allows you direct access to the raw HTML code if you want. This can be an advantage for people who know HTML and want to do some formatting of their page by typing tags. In Dreamweaver, Code view mode, Code Inspector, and Quick Tag Editor enable you to edit your page by adding HTML information manually. Access to the code also means that you can add HTML features that Dreamweaver may not yet support.

Work in Design View and Code View

You can switch to Code view in the Document window to inspect and edit the HTML code and other code on the Web page. You can use the Split view to see both the HTML code and Design view at the same time.

You will probably do most of your work in Design view, which displays your page approximately as it will appear in a Web browser.

Work in Design View and Code View

① In the Document window, click a code-viewing option.

You can click **Code view** (icon) to display the source code of your page in the Document window.

You can click **Split view** (icon) to split the window and display both your source code and the design in the Document window.

● You can click **Window** and then click **Code Inspector** to display the code in a separate window.

Both Code view and Design view appear in the Document window when you click **Split view** (icon).

● The HTML and other code appear in one pane.

● The Design view appears in the other pane.

② Click the code and type to edit the text, or to add or modify the HTML code.

The content in Design view automatically updates to reflect the code changes.

● Keep in mind that when you select text, an image, or any other element in the Design view, it is automatically highlighted in Code view.

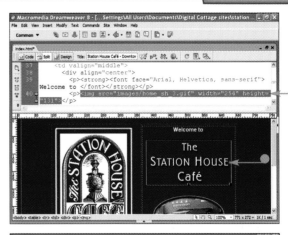

③ Click in the Design view window and type to make changes.

● The content in the Code view updates dynamically as you make your changes.

TIP

How do I turn on line numbers in Code view or make code wrap at the right edge of the window?

You can access both of these options, as well as others, by clicking the **Options** button at the top of the Document window when you are in Code view.

Word Wrap
Line Numbers
Highlight Invalid
Syntax Coloring
Auto Indent

You define the basic structure of every HTML document with several basic tags. To view the HTML of a Web page, you can click the Code view button in the Document window, or you can click Window and then click Code Inspector.

`<html>` Tags
Opening and closing `<html>` tags begin and end every HTML document.

`<head>` Tags
Opening and closing `<head>` tags surround descriptive and accessory information for a page. This includes `<title>` and `<meta>` tag content.

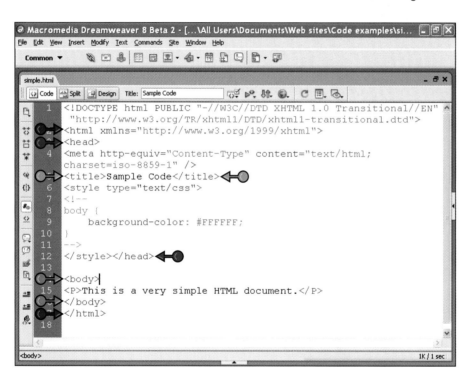

`<body>` Tags
Opening and closing `<body>` tags surround content that appears inside the Web browser window. For example, the `bgcolor` attribute of the `<body>` tag defines "`#FFFFFF`" as a hexadecimal color code that makes the background color white.

Page `<title>` Tags
Opening and closing `<title>` tags display the content in the Document window title bar.

Explore Block-Formatting Tags

You can organize information in your Web page with block-formatting tags. A block tag tells a Web browser to start a new line with the enclosed text. To view the HTML code of a Web page, you can click the Code view button in the Document window, or click Window and then click Code Inspector.

Code View

This page features HTML code with `<h>` heading, `<p>` paragraph, and `<ul>` unordered list tags.

Design View

This page features a heading, a paragraph, and an unordered list.

`<p>` Tag
The `<p>` tag organizes information into a paragraph.

`<ul>` and `<li>` Tags
The `<ul>` tag defines an unordered list. Each list item is defined with an `<li>` tag.

Heading Tag
An `<h>` tag creates a bold heading.

Paragraph Tag
A `<p>` tag separates a paragraph from other text.

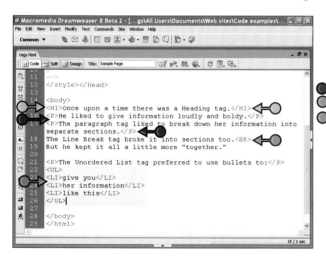

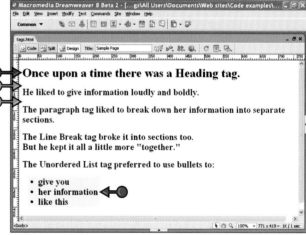

`<h>` Tag
An `<h>` tag organizes information into a heading. There are six levels of headings, `<h1>` (the largest) through `<h6>` (the smallest).

`<br>`, `<ol>`, and `<pre>` Tags
Other block-formatting tags include `<br>` (line break), `<ol>` (ordered list), and `<pre>` (preformatted text).

Unordered List Tag
A `<ul>` tag creates an unordered, bulleted list.

Explore
Text-Formatting Tags

You can format the style of sentences, words, and characters with text-formatting tags. Text formatting tags, also known as inline tags, tell a Web browser to format text without starting a new line. To view the HTML code of a Web page, you can click the Code view button in the Document window, or you can click Window and then click Code Inspector.

Code View

This page demonstrates the use of `<font>` font tags containing `size` and `color` attributes, `<b>` bold tags, and `<i>` italic tags.

Design View

This page features text with a different font size, as well as bold and italic text.

`<font>` Tag
The `<font>` tag controls various characteristics of text on a Web page.

`size` Attribute
The `size` attribute goes inside the `<font>` tag and specifies the size of text.

Font Size
The `size` attribute controls the text size.

Font Color
The `color` attribute controls the text color.

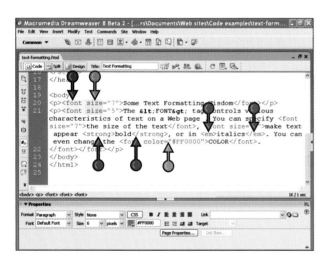

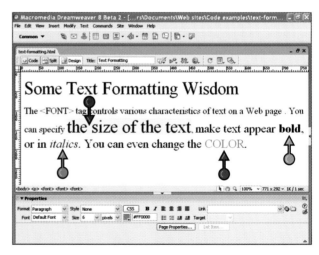

`color` Attribute
The `color` attribute also goes inside the `<font>` tag and specifies the color of text.

`<i>` Tag
The `<i>` tag defines text as italic.

`<b>` Tag
The `<b>` tag defines text as bold.

Italic Text
The `<i>` italic tag creates *italicized* text.

Bold Text
The `<b>` bold tag creates **bold** text.

You can add an image to your page with the `<img>` tag and then create a hyperlink with the `<a>` tag. To view the HTML code of a Web page, you can click the Code view button in the Document window, or you can click Window and then click Code Inspector.

Code View

This page demonstrates how to use `<img>` image and `<a>` hyperlink tags.

Design View

This page features a right-aligned image and a text hyperlink.

`<img>` Tag
The `<img>` tag inserts an image into a page.

src Attribute
The `src` attribute specifies an image file to insert.

Text Hyperlink
Clicking a hyperlink takes you to the linked document.

Right-Aligned Image
The image is placed as far right as possible.

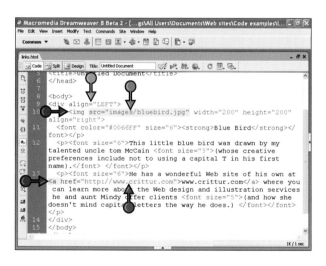

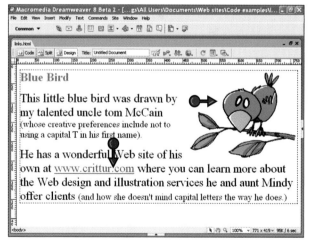

`<a>` Tag
The `<a>` tag specifies the content that will serve as a hyperlink.

align Attribute
The `align` attribute specifies the alignment of an image.

href Attribute
The `href` attribute specifies the hyperlink destination.

Clean Up
HTML Code

Dreamweaver can optimize the
HTML code in your Web page
by deleting redundant or non-
functional tags. This can
decrease the page file size and
make the source code easier to
read in Code view.

**It is a good idea to run the Clean Up
HTML command when editing
documents that were originally created
in other HTML editors, such as
FrontPage.**

Clean Up HTML Code

① Click 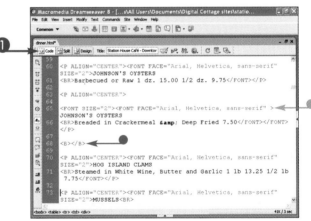 to view the HTML in Code view.

● In this example, multiple <font> tags appear in
the code, adding unnecessary code.

● In this example there is an empty <b> tag. Because
this tag serves no purpose, you can delete it.

② Click **Commands**.

③ Click **Clean Up HTML**.

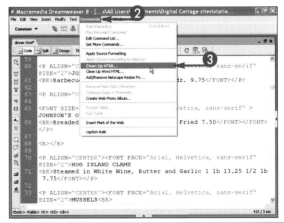

The Clean Up HTML/XHTML dialog box appears.

④ Click the clean up options that you want to remove
(☐ changes to ☑).

⑤ Click the clean up options that you want to select
(☐ changes to ☑).

⑥ Click **OK**.

● Dreamweaver parses the HTML and displays the
results, including a summary of what was removed.

⑦ Click **OK**.

● The cleaned-up HTML appears in the Document
window.

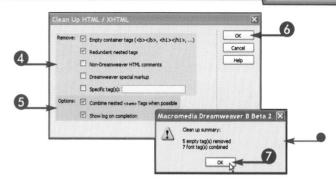

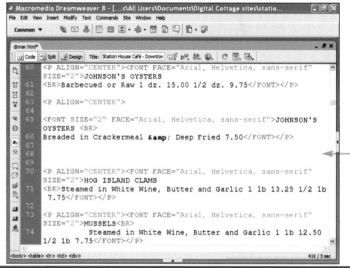

How do empty tags end up appearing in the Dreamweaver HTML?

Sometimes you may heavily edit Web-page text in the Document window, for example, by cutting and pasting sentences and reformatting words. In these cases, Dreamweaver inadvertently removes text from inside tags without removing the tags themselves.

Does Dreamweaver fix invalid HTML?

By default, Dreamweaver rewrites some instances of invalid HTML. When you open an HTML document, Dreamweaver rewrites tags that are not nested properly, closes tags that are not allowed to remain open, and removes extra closing tags. If Dreamweaver does not recognize a tag, it highlights it in red and displays it in the Document window, but it does not remove the tag. You can change or turn off this behavior by clicking **Edit**, then clicking **Preferences**, and then selecting the category **Code Rewriting**.

View and Edit Head Content

Dreamweaver gives you various ways to view, add to, and edit the head content of a Web page. For example, Meta tags store special descriptive information about the page for use by search engines.

View and Edit Head Content

INSERT HEAD CONTENT

1 Click here and select **HTML**.

● Information on the head content appears in the Properties inspector.

In this example, the `<Title>` information displays in the Properties inspector.

● The HTML options appear in the Insert panel.

2 Click the **Head** ⊡ and select a content button.

This example uses the Description button (⊞).

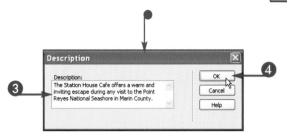

● A Description dialog box appears.

❸ Type a description for your page.

If you selected the Keywords content button in Step **2**, then type a series of keywords, separated by commas.

❹ Click **OK**.

● The new head content is automatically inserted into the code of the page.

To view the HTML code for the new head content, click .

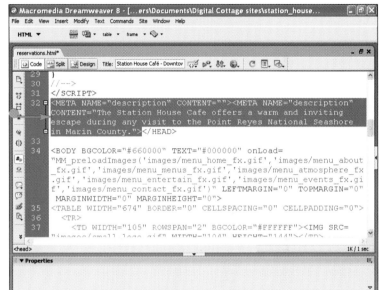

How can I influence how search engines rank my pages?

Search engines work by organizing the important information found in Web pages into a searchable database. Many search engines give greater importance to the description and keyword information that you add to the head content of HTML documents. Short of paying for high-ranking placement, you can influence how a search engine ranks your pages by adding concise descriptions and relevant keywords to the head content of each page that you create.

Access Reference Information About HTML Tags

You can get quick access to reference information about HTML tags and their attributes by using the Reference tab in the Code panel. You can also insert short pieces of pre-written HTML code from the Snippets panel.

Use the Reference Panel

① Click 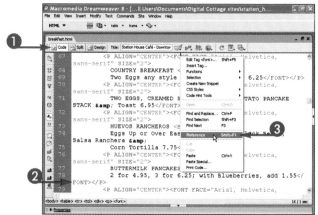 to display the HTML code of the page.

② Click and drag to select an HTML tag.

Note: It is not necessary to select the entire tag.

③ Right-click a tag in the document and select Reference from the pop-up menu.

● The Reference panel opens, containing a description of the HTML tag.

● You can click here and select a tag attribute.

● Information appears on the attribute.

● You can click here to look up a different HTML tag.

● You can click here to find information about JavaScript objects or style sheet rules.

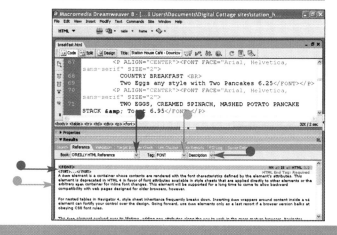

Use the Snippets Panel

① Click in the HTML document where you want to insert a code snippet.

② Click **Window**.

③ Click **Snippets**.

● The Snippets panel appears.

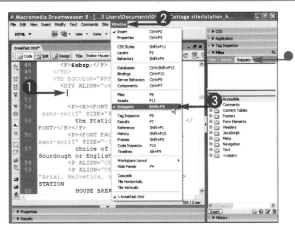

④ Click the expand button (⊞) next to one of the code options, such as **Navigation**, to expand the folder structure (⊞ changes to ⊟).

⑤ Double-click **Bullet as Separator**.

● A navigation row with pseudo-Latin filler text appears in the selected area of your document.

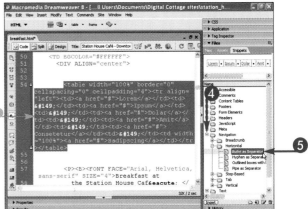

TIPS

Does Dreamweaver have commands for creating all of the tags listed in the Reference panel?

With Dreamweaver's commands, you can create most of the tags listed in the Reference panel, especially frequently used tags. However, there are tags listed for which Dreamweaver does not offer commands. For example, you cannot insert the Navigation options with any of Dreamweaver's table commands.

What does the text Lorem ipsum dolor mean that appears in Web pages?

The text is actually dummy text used as a placeholder when laying out pages. Although this text appears all over the Internet as placeholder text, its meaning has nothing to do with its usage. Many designers use Latin or other text that has no meaning in English to represent areas where text will be added later. The theory is that using Latin text will make it obvious that the text still needs to be replaced.

5

Formatting and Styling Text

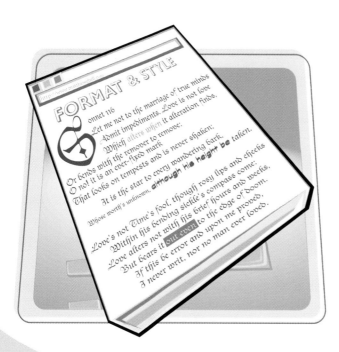

Text is the easiest type of information to add to a Web page using Dreamweaver. This chapter shows you how to create headlines, paragraphs, bulleted lists, and stylized text.

When you format text with heading tags, you can create large, bold text and specify a range of sizes. You can also align your heading text.

Create a Heading

① Click and drag to select the text.

② Click the **Format** ▾ in the Properties inspector.

③ Click a heading level.

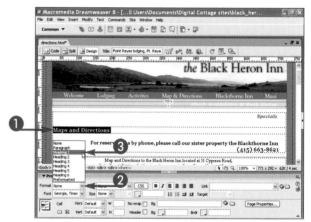

● The font size is larger, and the text is now bold. White space separates it from other text.

④ Click and drag to select more text.

⑤ Click the **Format** ▾.

⑥ Click a different heading.

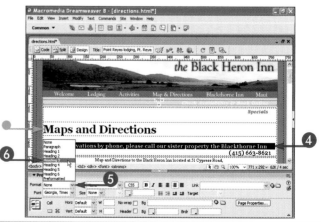

● The second heading appears different from the first, but still bold.

Note: *The higher the heading number, the smaller the text formatting.*

⑦ Click and drag to select the heading text.

⑧ Click an alignment option to align your heading.

You can choose to align left (≡), center (≡), align right (≡), and justify (≡).

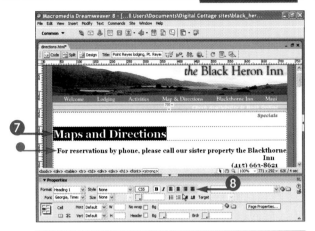

The heading text aligns on the page.

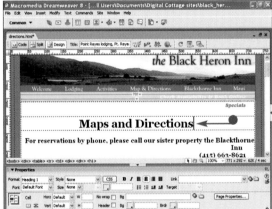

TIPS

What heading levels should I use to format my text?

Headings 1, 2, and 3 are often used for titles and subtitles. Heading 4 is similar to a bold version of default text. Headings 5 and 6 are often used for copyright and disclaimer information in small page footers.

Why are my headlines different sizes when I see them on another computer?

Size can vary from one computer to the next because some users set their Web browsers to display larger or smaller type on their computer. Browsers use the default text size to determine the size of the heading. For example, Heading 1 text is three times larger than the default text size, and Heading 6 text is three times smaller.

Create Paragraphs

You can organize text on your Web page by creating and aligning paragraphs.

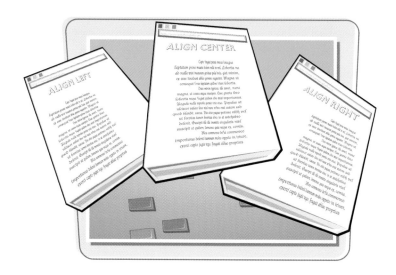

Create Paragraphs

① Type the text for your Web page into the Document window.

② Position the cursor where you want a paragraph break.

③ Press **Enter** (**Return**).

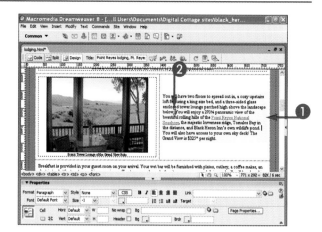

● A blank line appears between the blocks of text, separating the text into paragraphs.

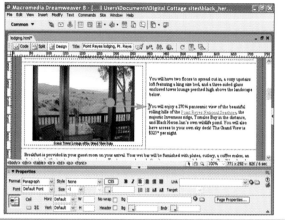

Note: Paragraphs align left by default.

④ Click and drag to select the paragraph that you want to align.

⑤ Click an alignment option to align your paragraph.

You can choose to align left (▤), center (▤), align right (▤), and justify (▤).

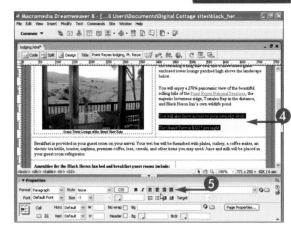

● The paragraph aligns on the page.

TIPS

What controls the width of the paragraphs on my Web page?

The width of your paragraphs depends on the width of the Web browser window. When a user changes the size of the browser window, the widths of the paragraphs also change. In this way, the user can always view all of the text in the paragraph. You can also use tables to further control the width of your paragraphs. For more on tables, see Chapter 9.

What is the HTML code for paragraphs?

In HTML, paragraphs are distinguished by opening and closing <p> tags. You can click the **Code view** button (▣) to view the HTML code of the page.

Create
Line Breaks

When you do not want a full paragraph break, you can use line breaks to keep lines of text adjacent. When you hold down the Shift key and press Enter (or Return for a Mac), you create a line break.

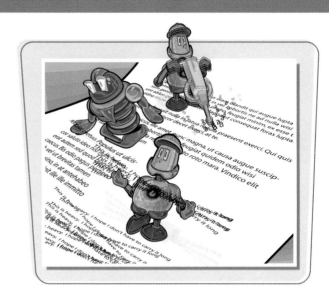

Create Line Breaks

① Click where you want the line of text to break.

② Press Shift + Enter (Shift + Return).

● Dreamweaver adds a line break.

Note: *You can combine paragraph and line breaks to add more space between lines of text.*

You can make selected paragraphs stand out from the rest of the text on your Web page by indenting them. For example, indents are often used for displaying quotations.

Indent Paragraphs

1 Click and drag to select a paragraph.

2 Click 🔳 to indent the text.

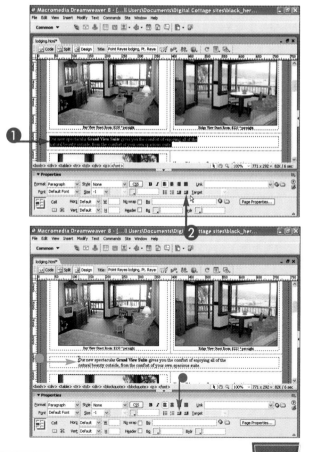

● Additional space appears in both the left and right margins of the paragraph.

You can repeat Steps **1** and **2** to indent a paragraph further.

● You can outdent an indented paragraph by clicking 🔳.

Create Lists

You can organize text items into unordered lists. Unordered lists have items that are indented and bulleted, and not listed by numbers or letters.

Create Unordered Lists

1. Type your list items into the Document window.

2. Click between the items and press **Enter** (**Return**) to place each item in a separate paragraph.

3. Click and drag to select all of the list items.

4. Click **Unordered List** (📇) in the Properties inspector.

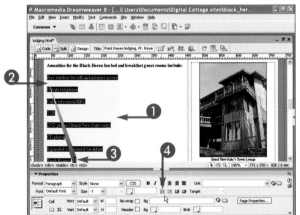

● The list items appear indented and bulleted.

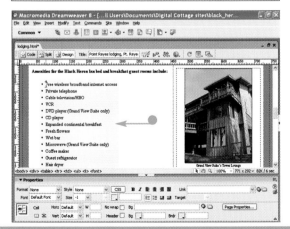

Create Ordered Lists

① Type your list items into the Document window.

② Click between the items and press `Enter` (`Return`) to place each item in a separate paragraph.

③ Click and drag to select all of the list items.

④ Click **Ordered List** (☷) in the Properties inspector.

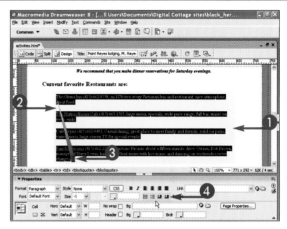

● The list items appear indented and numbered.

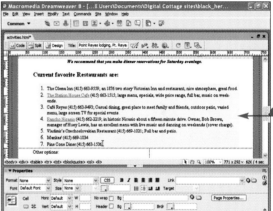

TIPS

Can I modify the appearance of my unordered list?

You can modify the style of an unordered list by highlighting an item in the list and clicking **Text**, then clicking **List**, and then clicking **Properties**. The dialog box that appears enables you to select different bullet styles for your unordered list.

Can I modify the appearance of my ordered list?

You can modify the style of an ordered list by highlighting an item in the list and clicking **Text**, then clicking **List**, and then clicking **Properties**. The dialog box that appears enables you to select different numbering schemes for your ordered list.

Insert Special Characters

You can insert special characters into your Web page that do not appear on your keyboard.

INSERT CHARACTERS

1. Click the **Insert panel** ☑ and select **Text**.

2. Click where you want to insert the special character.

3. Click **Characters menu** (☐ ▾).

4. Click the special character that you want to insert.

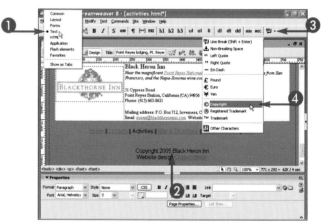

● The special character appears in your Web page text.

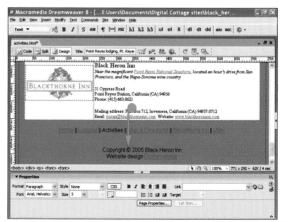

INSERT OTHER CHARACTERS

1 Click **Characters menu** (BRJ ·).

2 Click **Other Characters** (⊞).

The Insert Other Character dialog box appears, displaying a wider variety of special characters.

3 Click a special character.

The HTML code that defines that special character is inserted into the HTML code of the page.

4 Click **OK**.

● The special character appears in your Web page text.

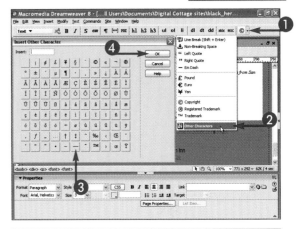

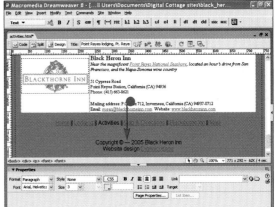

TIPS

How do I include non-English language text on my Web page?

Many foreign languages feature accented characters that do not appear on standard keyboards. You can insert most of these characters using the special characters feature described in this section.

Why do special characters look strange in a browser?

Although most Web browsers display double quotation marks without problems, some standard punctuation marks are considered special characters and require special code. If you do not use the special HTML code, those characters may not display properly.

Change the Font Face

For aesthetic purposes or to emphasize certain elements on your Web pages, you can change the font style of your text.

You can customize the fonts on your Web pages by using style sheets, also called Cascading Style Sheets or CSS. For more information about style sheets, see Chapter 7.

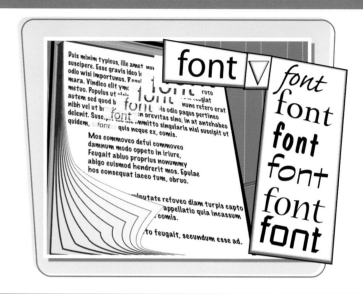

Change the Font Face

CHANGE THE FONT

① Click and drag to select the text.

② Click the **Font** ☑ in the Properties inspector.

③ Click a font.

● The text changes to the new font.

You can create a new style in Dreamweaver and apply it by using the Properties inspector.

Note: To find out how to create styles, see Chapter 7.

ADD AN ENTRY TO THE FONT MENU

① Click **Text**.

② Click **Font**.

③ Click **Edit Font List**.

The Edit Font List dialog box appears.

● The fonts that appear in the Font menu display in this area.

● The fonts installed on your computer appear in the Available Fonts list.

④ Click a font.

⑤ Click the **Add Font** arrows to add the font.

⑥ Click **OK**.

● The new font appears in the Font menu.

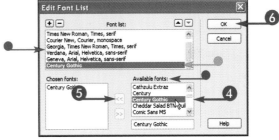

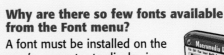

How are fonts classified?

The two most common categories of fonts are serif and sans-serif. Serif fonts are distinguished by the decorations, or serifs, that make the ends of their lines curly. Common serif fonts include Times New Roman, Palatino, and Garamond. Sans-serif fonts lack these decorations and have straight edges. Common sans-serif fonts include Arial, Verdana, and Helvetica.

Why are there so few fonts available from the Font menu?

A font must be installed on the user's computer to display in a Web browser. Dreamweaver's default list of fonts specifies the common typefaces that are available on most computers, and alternate styles if the user does not have those fonts installed. If you want to use an unusual font, then you should convert the text to a graphic.

You can change the size of your text by using the font size tag. Unlike the heading tags, when you apply the font size tag, Dreamweaver does not add a paragraph return.

Change the Font Size

① Click and drag to select the text.

② Click the **Size** ☑ in the Properties inspector.

③ Click a font size.

● The size of the text changes.

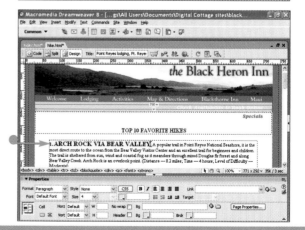

Change the Font Color

You can change the color of text on all or part of your Web page. You should ensure that it is readable and complements the background.

Change the Font Color

① Click and drag to select the text that you want to change.

② Click the **Color Swatch** (▣) in the Properties inspector (↳ changes to ✐).

The Color Palette appears.

③ Click a color.

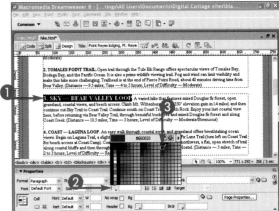

● The selected text appears in the new color.

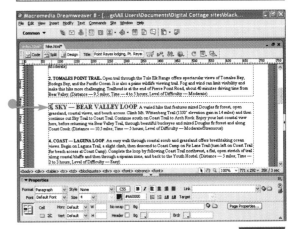

Change Text, Link, and Page Colors

You can change the link, text, and background colors for the entire page in the Page Properties dialog box.

Change the Background Color of a Page

① Click **Modify**.

② Click **Page Properties**.

The Page Properties dialog box appears.

③ Click the **Background Color Swatch** (■).

The Color Palette appears.

④ Click any color to select it.

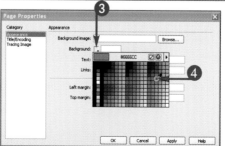

⑤ Click **Apply** to see the color change on the page.

⑥ Click the **Text Color Swatch** (🔲).

The Color Palette appears.

⑦ Click any color to select it.

⑧ Click **Apply**.

⑨ Click **OK** to close the dialog box.

Your text appears in the new color on your Web page.

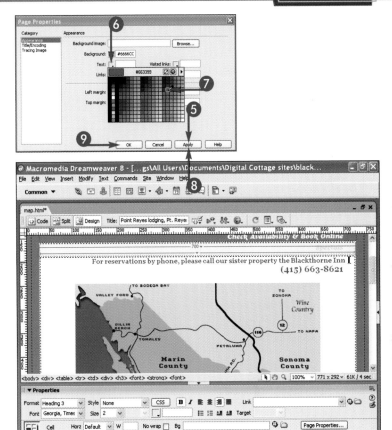

What are the letter and number combinations that appear in the color fields of Dreamweaver?

HTML represents colors using six-digit codes called *hexadecimal codes*, or hex codes. These codes represent the amount of red, green, and blue used to create a particular color, and are preceded by a pound sign (#). Instead of ranging from 0 to 9, hex-code digits range from 0 to F, with A equal to 10, B equal to 11, and so on through F, which is equal to 15. The first two digits in the hex code specify the amount of red in the selected color. The second two digits specify the amount of green, and the third two digits specify the amount of blue.

#FFFFFF

#FFCCFF

#FF6600

#99CC00

#0099CC

#000000

Import Text from Another Document

You can save time by importing text from an existing document, instead of typing it all over again. This is particularly convenient when you have tabular data that needs to appear in a table. By importing a comma- or tab-delimited text file, you do not have to re-create the entire table in HTML. Dreamweaver creates it automatically.

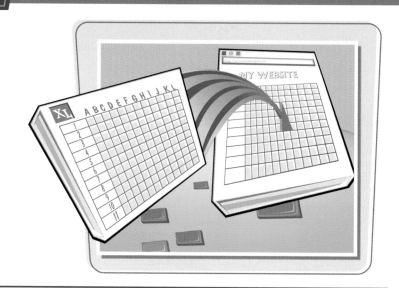

IMPORT AN EXCEL DOCUMENT

1 Click **File**.

2 Click **Import**.

3 Click **Excel Document**.

The Import Excel Document dialog box appears.

4 Click here and select the file you want to import.

5 Click the file.

6 Click **Open**.

The content from the imported Excel document appears in the Document window. Tables and other formatting from Excel are translated into HTML in Dreamweaver.

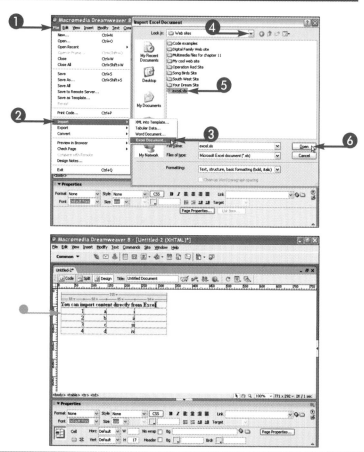

IMPORT A WORD DOCUMENT

1 Click **File**.

2 Click **Import**.

3 Click **Word Document**.

The Import Word Document dialog box appears.

4 Click here and select the file that you want to import.

5 Click the file.

6 Click **Open**.

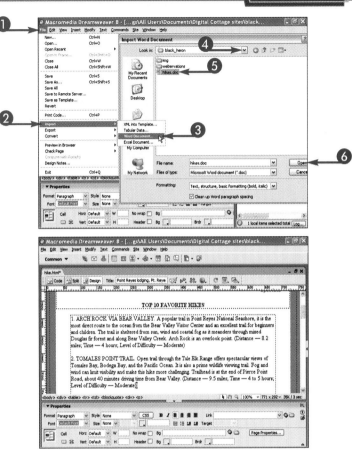

The imported Word document appears in the Document window. The formatting from Word is translated into HTML.

When is it a good idea to import text?

Even if you type at speeds of over 100 words per minute, you can save time if you do not have to retype all of your documents. If your original text file was created using a word processing program such as Microsoft Word, then you can speed up the process by importing the Word document into Dreamweaver. When you import Excel documents, Dreamweaver builds tables to duplicate the formatting from Excel. Once you have imported the documents, you can edit and format text, and add images, tables, and multimedia as you normally would.

CHAPTER 6

Working with Images and Multimedia

www.suburbansasquatch.com

You can make your Web page much more interesting by adding digital photos, scanned art, animation, and interactive visual elements. This chapter shows you how to insert and format these elements.

Insert an Image into a Web Page

You can insert different types of images into your Web page, including clip art, digital camera images, and scanned photos. You must first save the images in a Web format, such as GIF or JPEG.

Insert an Image into a Web Page

① Click to position the mouse ↳ where you want to insert the image.

② Click **Insert**.

③ Click **Image**.

You can also click **Image** (🖻) in the Common Insert bar.

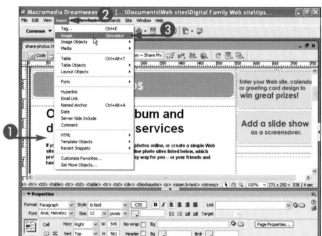

The Select Image Source dialog box appears.

④ Click here and select the folder that contains the image.

⑤ Click the image file that you want to insert into your Web page.

● A preview of the image appears.

● You can insert an image that exists at an external Web address by typing the address into the URL field.

⑥ Click **OK**.

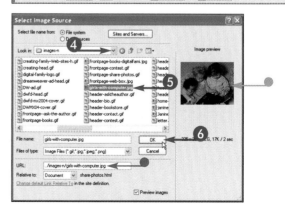

● The image appears where you positioned your cursor in the Web page.

To delete an image, click the image and press `Delete`.

ADD A BORDER TO AN IMAGE

① Click an image to select it.

② Type the width into the Border field.

This example uses a border of 2 pixels.

③ Press `Enter` (`Return`).

A black border appears around the image. If the image is a link, the border appears in the link color.

Note: To learn how to change link colors, see Chapter 5.

What file formats can you use for Web images?

The majority of the images that you see on Web pages are GIF and JPEG files. Both GIF and JPEG are compressed file formats, which means that they are smaller than other image files and therefore download faster. The GIF format is best for images that have a limited number of colors, such as cartoons or line art. The JPEG format is best for photographs and other images with millions of colors. You can insert both GIF and JPEG files into your Web page using the steps described in this section.

Wrap Text Around an Image

You can wrap text around an image by aligning the image to one side of a Web page. Wrapping text around images enables you to fit more information onto the screen, and gives your Web pages a more finished, professional look. There are many alignment options, and you may want to experiment to find the best effect for your page.

Wrap Text Around an Image

① Click an image to select it.

② Click the **Align** ☑.

③ Click an alignment for the image.

● The text flows around the image according to the alignment that you selected.

In this example, the text flows to the right of the left-aligned image.

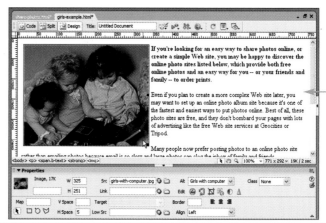

- You can select other options from the Align ☑ menu for different wrapping effects, such as Right or Middle.

- In this example, the text flows to the left of the right-aligned image.

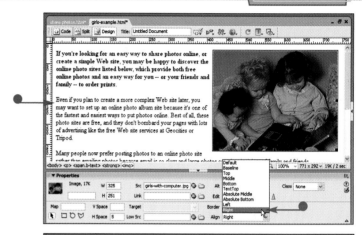

- In this example, the text aligns to the middle of the image.

How can I determine the download time for my Web page?

The total size of your Web page appears in kilobytes (K) on the status bar. The total size includes the size of your HTML file, the size of your images, and the size of any other elements on the Web page. Next to the size is the estimated download time for the Web page.

What is the ideal size of a Web page?

Most Web designers feel comfortable putting up a page with a total size under 100K. However, there are exceptions to this rule. For example, you may want to break this rule for an especially important image file. The 100K limit does not apply to multimedia files, although multimedia files should be kept as small as possible.

Align an Image

The alignment of an image can give a photo or banner prominence on your Web page. Depending on the layout of your Web page, you can center an image or align it left or right.

① Click to place the mouse ⌖ to the immediate right of the image.

② Press **Enter** (**Return**) to place the image on its own line.

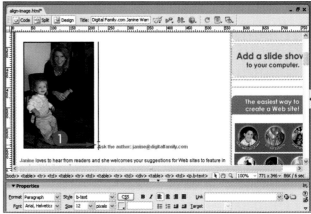

③ Click the image to select it.

④ Click ▤.

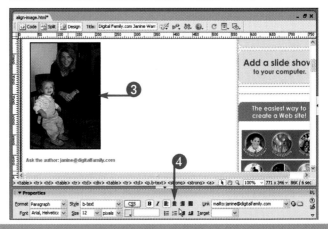

- The image appears in the center of the page.

- Using the alignment tools to align the image does not influence the text wrapping around the image.

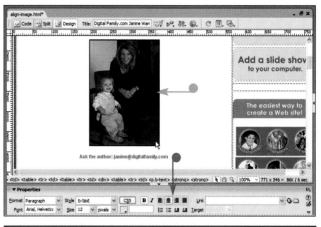

- You can align the image to the right side of the page by clicking  or align the image to the left side by clicking .

TIP

How can I use centered images to enhance my text?

You can create custom graphics or icons in an image-editing program, and then use these images as visual elements on your Web page. You can use small, centered icons to divide main sections of text in your Web page. These icons serve the same purpose as horizontal rules, but add a more sophisticated look to your Web pages.

Crop an Image

You can trim, or crop, an image by using the Crop tool and dragging the crop handles to adjust how much of the image you want to show. This can be handy for quick edits without using an external image-editing program, as it physically crops the image file.

① Click an image to select it.

② Click the **Crop tool** (⬚).

● A dialog box appears.

● You can turn off this warning by checking the option box (☐ changes to ☑).

③ Click **OK**.

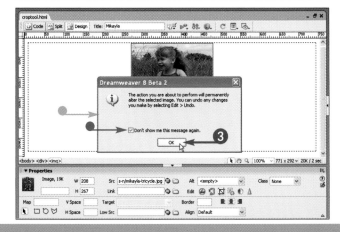

④ Click and drag the black square handles to define the area that you want to crop.

The part of the photo that appears grayed out will delete.

⑤ Double-click inside the crop box.

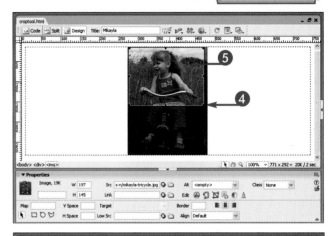

● The image trims to the size of the crop box.

Keep in mind that when you save the page, the image is permanently cropped.

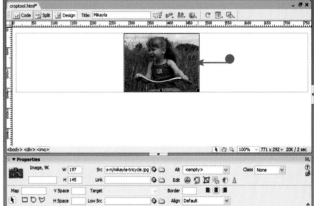

Should I edit images in Dreamweaver or use an external graphics program?

Macromedia has added the Crop tool to make working on a Web page faster and easier. If you need to do a simple crop, the Crop tool is faster than opening the image in an image-editing program like Macromedia Fireworks or Adobe Photoshop. However, if you want to save a copy of the original before you make the crop, or do other image editing, then you need to use a dedicated image-editing program.

Resize an Image

You can change the display size of an image without changing the file size of the image. You can do this by using a percentage, a pixel size, or by clicking and dragging the corner of the image.

Pixels are tiny, solid-color squares that make up a digital image and are useful for making specific size changes.

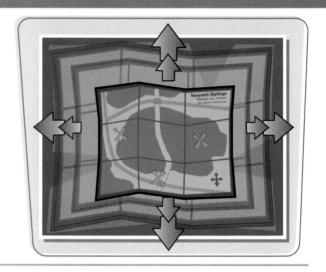

Resize an Image

CHANGE THE PIXEL OR PERCENTAGE DIMENSIONS TO RESIZE

1 Click an image to select it.

● The dimensions of the image appear.

2 Type the desired width of the image, either in pixels or as a percentage.

Instead of pixels, you can type a percentage of the window or table cell for the width and height. For example, you can type **50%** in both fields to make the image half the size of the window or table cell.

3 Press **Enter** (**Return**).

4 Type the desired height of the image in pixels or as a percentage.

5 Press **Enter** (**Return**).

● The image displays with its new dimensions.

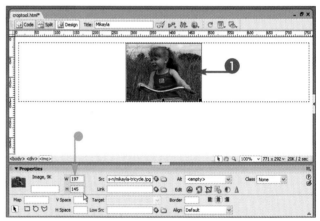

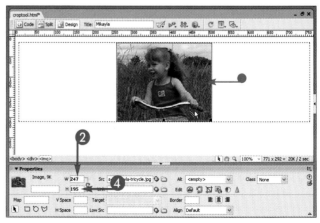

CLICK AND DRAG TO RESIZE

1 Click an image to select it.

2 Drag one of the handles at the edge of the image (handle changes to ↘).

To resize the image proportionally, press and hold Shift as you drag a corner.

The image expands or contracts to the new size.

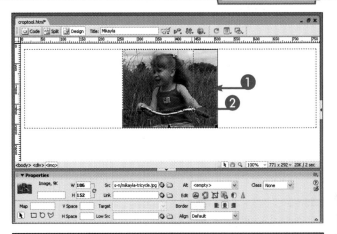

RESET THE IMAGE TO THE ORIGINAL SIZE

If you want, you can reset the image to its original size.

1 Click the image to select it.

2 Click **Reset Size** (🖳) in the Properties inspector.

The image returns to its original size.

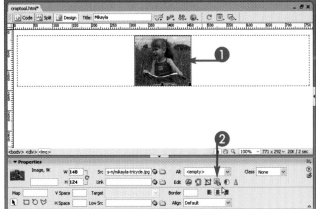

What is the best way to change the dimensions of an image on a Web page?

Although you can change the pixel dimensions or click and drag an image in Dreamweaver to stretch or shrink it on the Web page, this does not actually resize the image's true dimensions. Clicking and dragging an image may cause distortion or alter proportions. A better way to resize an image is to open it in an image editor such as Macromedia Fireworks, and change its physical size.

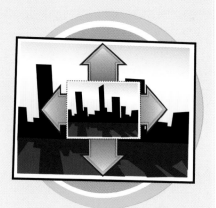

Open an Image in Fireworks

Macromedia designed Fireworks to work in tandem with Dreamweaver so that you can easily open and edit images while you are working on your Web pages. Fireworks is a sophisticated image-editing program that allows you to make many changes to an image.

Although you can use any image editor, Fireworks is integrated with Dreamweaver because Macromedia makes both programs.

Open an Image in Fireworks

① Click an image to select it in Dreamweaver.

You can open any image in an external editor from within Dreamweaver.

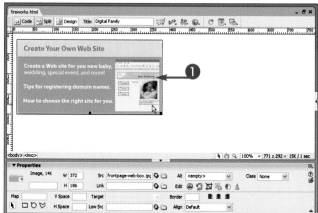

② Click **Fireworks** (⊚) in the Properties inspector.

You may have to wait a few moments while Fireworks opens.

In Dreamweaver's preferences, you can associate other image editors, such as Adobe Photoshop.

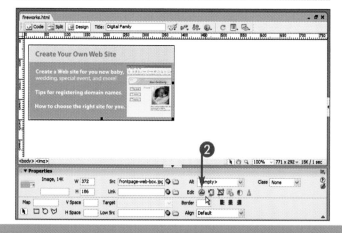

The image opens in the Fireworks window.

You can edit the image in Fireworks.

③ Click **File**.

④ Click **Save**.

Your changes to the image become permanent.

● The image saves and automatically updates in the Dreamweaver window.

To edit the image again or to edit another image, select the image and repeat Steps **2** to **4**.

What can you do in an image-editing program?

A program like Fireworks or Adobe Photoshop allows you to edit and combine images to create almost anything that you can imagine.

If you have Fireworks installed, then you can open it to edit an image directly from Dreamweaver. In the Properties inspector, click the **Edit/Fireworks Logo** button (📷).

Add Space Around an Image

You can add space around an image to separate it from the text and other images on your Web page. This creates a cleaner page layout.

ADD SPACE TO THE LEFT AND RIGHT OF AN IMAGE

① Click an image to select it.

② Type an amount in the H Space field.

③ Press **Enter** (**Return**).

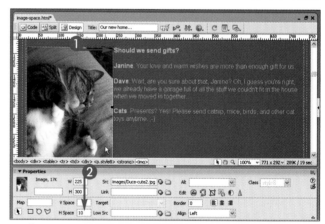

● Extra space appears to the left and right of the image.

ADD SPACE ABOVE AND BELOW AN IMAGE

1 Click the image to select it.

2 Type an amount in the V Space field.

3 Press Enter (Return).

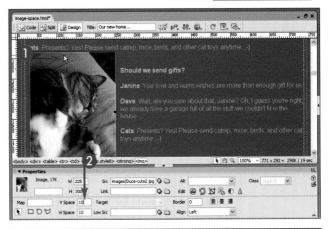

● Extra space appears above and below the image.

Is there any other way to add space around my image?

In many cases, adding space around your images enhances the appearance of your Web page. The extra space makes text easier to read and keeps adjacent images from appearing as a single image. However, when you add space using the horizontal and vertical space options in Dreamweaver, you add space to all sides of the image. If you only want to create space on one side, you can edit the image in a program like Fireworks or Adobe Photoshop to increase the canvas size of the image. This adds an invisible border on whichever side you choose.

Add a Background Image

You can incorporate a background image to add texture to your Web page. Background images appear beneath any text or images that are on your Web page, and are repeated across and down the Web browser window.

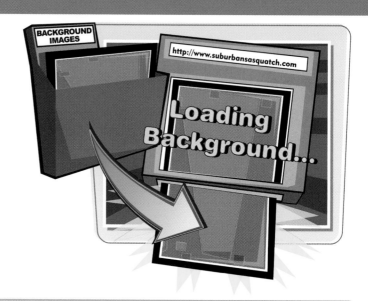

① Click **Page Properties** in the Properties inspector.

The Page Properties dialog box appears.

② Click **Appearance**.

③ Click **Browse**.

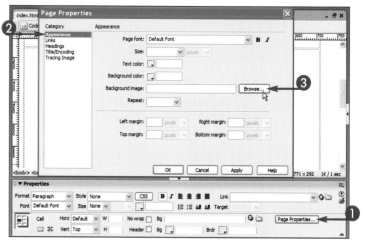

The Select Image Source dialog box appears.

④ Click here select the folder that contains the background image file.

⑤ Click the background image that you want to insert.

● A preview image appears.

⑥ Click **OK**.

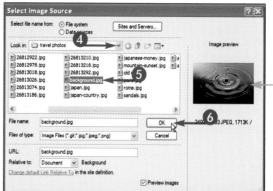

● The image filename and path appear in the Background image text field.

⑦ Click **OK**.

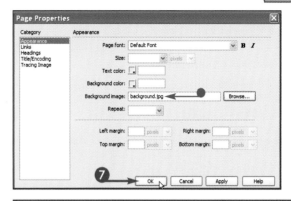

The image appears as a background on the Web page.

Note: If necessary, the image tiles horizontally and vertically to fill the entire window. You can resize the image in an image editor to adjust its appearance.

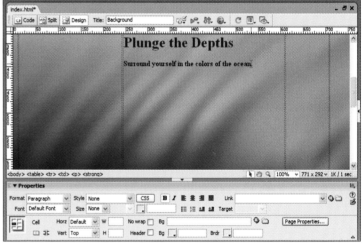

What types of images make good backgrounds?

Textures, subtle patterns, and photos with large open areas all make good background images. It is important to make sure that the image does not clash with the text and other content in the foreground, or overwhelm the rest of the page. Using an image that tiles seamlessly is also a good idea so that your background appears to be one large image that covers the entire page.

Are backgrounds always patterns?

Although many backgrounds repeat a pattern of some kind, a background image can also be an image that is big enough to fill the entire screen. Because a background image tiles, a vertical image creates a stripe across the top of the page, and a horizontal image creates a left-hand stripe.

Change the Background Color

You can add color to your Web pages by changing the background color. Dreamweaver offers a selection of Web-safe colors that are designed to display well on all computer monitors.

Change the Background Color

Change the Background Color

① Click **Page Properties** in the Properties inspector.

The Page Properties dialog box appears.

② Click **Appearance**.

③ Click the **Background color** 🔲 to open the color menu (↳ changes to ✐).

④ Click a color from the menu using the **Eyedropper tool** (✐).

⑤ Click **OK**.

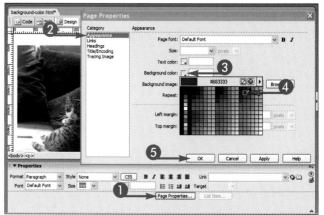

The background of your Web page displays in the color that you selected.

Note: For additional information about Web color, see Chapter 5.

Add Alternate
Text to an Image

You can add alternate text for users to read when they place their mouse over an image, or if an image does not appear on your page.

Some Web browsers cannot display images, and some users view Web pages with images turned off. The Alt image feature is also important to the visually impaired and others who use Web browsers that "read" Web pages.

Add Alternate Text to an Image

1 Click an image to select it.

2 Type the desired text in the Alt field.

3 Press Enter (Return).

The alternate text appears when users roll a mouse over the image in a Web browser that supports alternate text, such as Internet Explorer.

Note: *Alternate text also displays when a Web browser does not load images.*

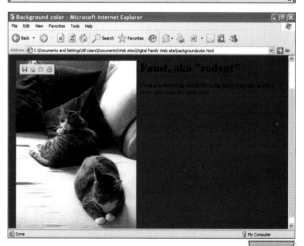

Insert a Flash File

You can add life to your Web page by adding Flash animations and movies. A Flash file is a multimedia file that is created with Macromedia Flash software. Flash files are used for both informational and entertainment purposes, including animated banner ads, cartoons, e-learning content, interactive animations, and site navigation.

Insert a Flash File

① Position the mouse ⮝ where you want to insert a Flash movie.

② Click **Insert**.

③ Click **Media**.

④ Click **Flash**.

The Select File dialog box appears.

⑤ Click here and select the folder that contains the Flash movie.

Note: *Flash movie filenames end with a .swf extension.*

⑥ Click the file that you want to insert into your Web page.

⑦ Click **OK**.

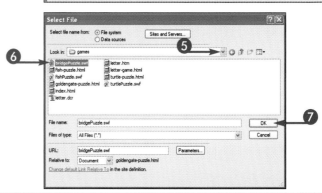

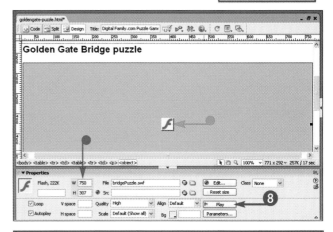

chapter 6

● The Flash plug-in icon appears in the Document window.

● You can change the size of the Flash movie by clicking and dragging its lower-left corner, or by entering a width and height in the Properties inspector.

⑧ Click **Play** (Play) in the Properties inspector to test the Flash movie.

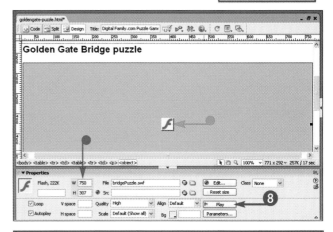

● The Flash movie displays in your Dreamweaver document.

● You can click the **Quality** and select the level of quality at which you want your movie to play. The higher the quality, the better it displays, but the longer it takes to download.

TIP

What are good uses for Flash on the Web?
Flash is an ideal tool for creating animations, interactive games, and other high-end features. You can even integrate video and audio files to create rich multimedia features for your Web site. You can learn more about Flash and see many examples at www.macromedia.com.

Insert Other Multimedia Files

You can add video, audio, and other multimedia to your Web pages in a wide variety of formats.

Insert other Multimedia Files

① Position the mouse ⫯ where you want to insert the multimedia file in the Document window.

② Click **Insert**.

③ Click **Media**.

④ Click **Plugin**.

When you add a video or sound clip to a Web page, Web browsers are able to handle it by using special add-ons called plug-ins.

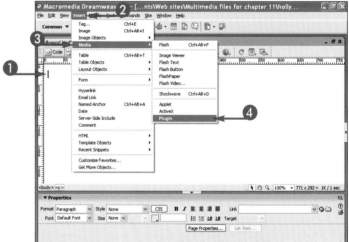

The Select File dialog box appears.

⑤ Click here and select the folder that contains the multimedia file.

⑥ Click the multimedia file that you want to insert into your Web page.

⑦ Click **OK**.

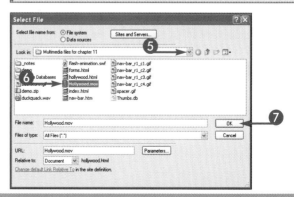

● A plug-in icon appears in the Document window.

⑧ Type the dimensions of the file in the W (width) and H (height) fields.

⑨ Type the URL of the Web site from which the user can download the plug-in.

If the plug-in is not installed on a user's Web browser, the browser asks whether the user wants to visit the site to download the plug-in.

⑩ Click to test the multimedia file in a browser.

⑪ Click your browser.

Some multimedia files require special players for viewing with a Web browser.

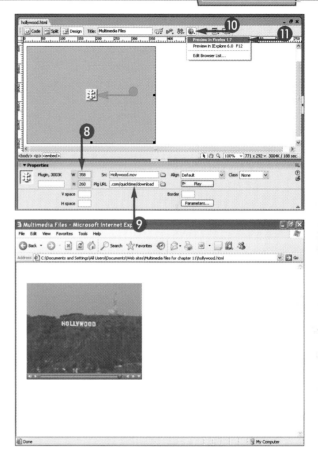

TIP

What should I know when adding multimedia content to my Web site?

Remember that although you may have the latest computer software and a fast connection, some of your visitors may not have the necessary multimedia players or bandwidth for your multimedia files. You can add Flash, video, sound, and other multimedia files to jazz up a Web site, but if your visitors do not have the right programs, then they cannot view them. Therefore it is very important to use compression and other techniques to keep file sizes low, and to offer links to players for any multimedia that you use.

Create a Rollover Image

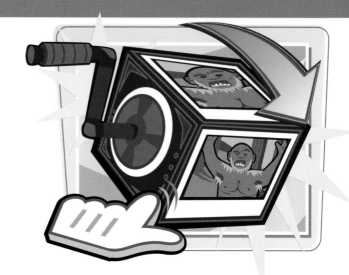

Rollover images are designed to react when someone rolls a cursor over them. They are commonly used in navigation bars and other links. The rollover effect can be subtle or dramatic, depending on the differences between the two images that you use in the rollover.

Create a Rollover Image

① Position the mouse ↖ where you want to insert the rollover image.

② Click **Insert**.

③ Click **Image Objects**.

④ Click **Rollover Image**.

The Insert Rollover Image dialog box appears.

⑤ Type an identifying name for scripting purposes.

⑥ Click **Browse**.

The Original Image dialog box appears.

⑦ Click here and select the folder that contains the image.

⑧ Click the image that you want to insert into your Web page.

⑨ Click **OK**.

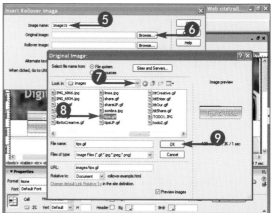

⑩ To select a rollover image, click **Browse** and repeat Steps **7** to **9**.

⑪ Type the URL of the page to which this image will link.

⑫ Click **OK**.

Dreamweaver automatically inserts the scripting that you need to make the rollover effect work.

● When you preview the page in a Web browser, the rollover image displays when the mouse ⇖ moves over the image. When the mouse ⇖ is removed, the original image reappears.

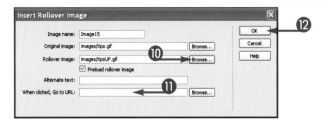

How does the rollover image work?

The interactive effect of a rollover image requires more than HTML. You can create this effect by using a scripting language called JavaScript. JavaScript is used for many kinds of interactivity, from calculators to pop-up windows. JavaScript is more complex than HTML code. Dreamweaver implements JavaScript through a feature that it calls behaviors. To see what other kinds of behaviors are available, use the Window menu to select the Behaviors panel.

Insert a Navigation Bar

You can increase the functionality of your Web site with a navigation bar. If your Web site consists of more than one page, then you can make it easier for your visitors to get around. A navigation bar is the best way to ensure that links to all of your main pages are available throughout your site.

① Position the mouse ⌖ where you want to insert the navigation bar.

② Click **Insert**.

③ Click **Image Objects**.

④ Click **Navigation Bar**.

The Insert Navigation Bar dialog box appears.

⑤ Type a name to identify the rollover in the script.

⑥ Click **Browse**.

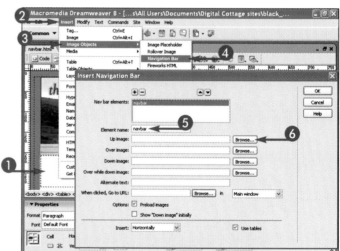

The Select image source dialog box appears.

⑦ Click here and select the folder that contains the image.

⑧ Click to select an Up image.

⑨ Click **OK**.

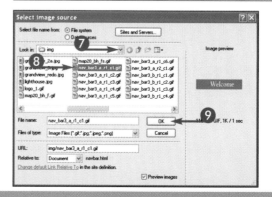

⑩ Repeat Steps **6** to **9** to select the Over, Down, and Over while down images.

Note: You may want to type some alternative text in case your images do not display.

⑪ Type the link for the navigation item.

⑫ Click ⊞ to add the navigation item.

⑬ To add additional navigation items, repeat Steps **5** to **12**.

⑭ Click **OK**.

● Dreamweaver automatically inserts the scripting that is needed to make the rollover effects work.

You can preview the page in a Web browser to see the rollover effects in action.

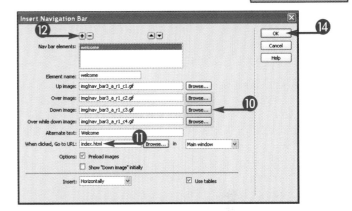

TIP

Where should I insert a navigation bar?

As a general rule, you want the navigation bar to be in the same place on every page. Most designers place them at the edge of a page where they cannot interfere with the design. It is common for Web pages to have left-hand navigation bars, especially for news Web sites or stores. However, horizontal navigation bars across the top or bottom of a page, and right-hand navigation bars are also acceptable. Horizontal navigation bars are somewhat limited by the available space across the Web browser window, but some designers use them in combination with side navigation bars to highlight sub-sections of a Web site. You can build a horizontal navigation bar by following Steps **1** to **4**, and then at the bottom of the Insert Navigation Bar dialog box, you simply click the **Insert** ▾ and then click **Horizontally**.

CHAPTER 7

Creating Hyperlinks

Links, also called hyperlinks, are used to connect related information. Using Dreamweaver, you can create links from one page to another in your Web site, or to other Web sites on the Internet, and you can also create e-mail links and image maps. This chapter shows you how to use both text and images as hyperlinks.

Link to Other Pages in Your Web Site

Dreamweaver allows you to create a link from one page in your Web site to another page, thus making it easy for visitors to navigate your Web site.

Link to Pages in Your Web Site

① Click and drag to select the text that you want to turn into a link.

Note: To link an image, see Chapter 6.

② Click the **Link** 🔲 in the Properties inspector.

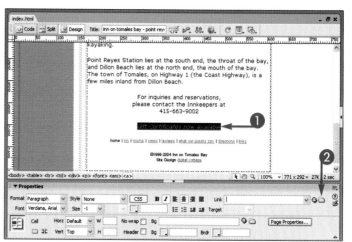

The Select File dialog box appears.

③ Click here and select the folder that contains the destination page.

④ Click the HTML file to which you want to link.

⑤ Click **OK**.

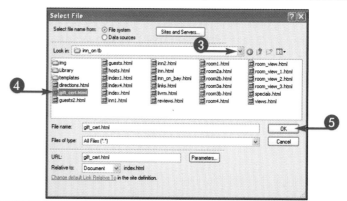

● The new link appears in color and underlined.

Note: Links are not clickable in the Document window.

● You can click test the link by previewing the file in a
Web browser, such as Firefox or Internet Explorer.

Note: For more on viewing a page in a Web browser, see Chapter 2.

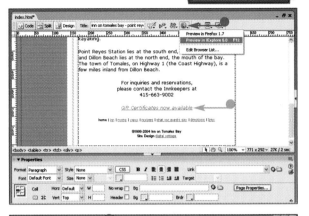

OPEN AND EDIT A LINKED PAGE

① Click anywhere on the text of the link whose
destination you want to open.

② Click **Modify**.

③ Click **Open Linked Page**.

The link destination opens in a Document window
allowing you to edit that document.

TIP

How should I organize the files that make up my Web site?
You should keep the files that make up your Web site in one main
folder that you define as your local site folder. This allows you to
easily find pages and images, and create links between your pages. It
also ensures that all of the links work correctly when you transfer the
files to a live Web server. If you have many pages under one section,
you can create subfolders to further divide the file structure of your
site. You may also want to create a separate file for images. For more
on setting up your Web site, see Chapter 2. For more on transferring
files to a Web server, see Chapter 14.

Link to Another Web Site

You can link from your Web site to any other Web site on the Internet, giving your visitors access to additional information and providing valuable references to related information.

Link to Another Web Site

① Click and drag to select the text that you want to turn into a link.

② Type the Web address of the destination page, including the **http://**, in the Link field in the Properties inspector.

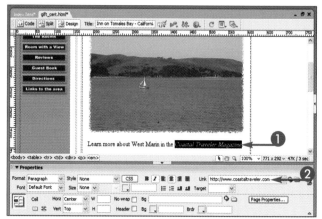

● The new link appears in a color and underlined.

Note: Links are not clickable in the Document window.

● You can test the link by previewing the file in a Web browser.

Note: To preview a Web page in a Web browser, see Chapter 2.

When you test the link in a Web browser while you are connected to the Internet, it should open the linked site, even if the link page is still on your hard drive.

REMOVE A LINK

① Select the text of the link that you want to remove.

② Click **Modify**.

③ Click **Remove Link**.

Dreamweaver removes the link, and the text no longer appears in a color and underlined.

How do I ensure that my links to other Web sites always work?

You do not have control over the Web pages on other Web sites to which you have linked. If you have linked to a Web page whose file is later renamed or taken offline, your viewers receive an error message when they click the link on your Web site. Maintain your Web site by periodically checking your links. You can also use software or Web site tune-up services, such as www.netmechanic.com to perform this check for you. Although neither single method can bring back a Web page that no longer exists, both methods combined can tell you which links you need to remove or update.

Use an Image as a Link

You can use an image to create a link to another page or Web site in much the same way that you create a link with text. Using images as links is a very common way to build a Web site's main navigation system, for example using a row of images that link to all of the main pages of the Web site.

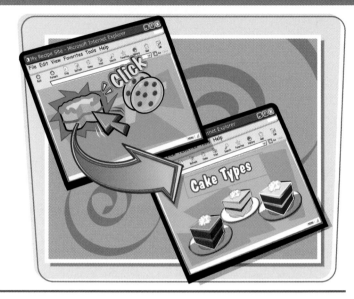

Use an Image as a Link

CREATE AN IMAGE LINK

1. Click the image that you want to turn into a link.

2. Click the **Link** 🔲 in the Properties inspector.

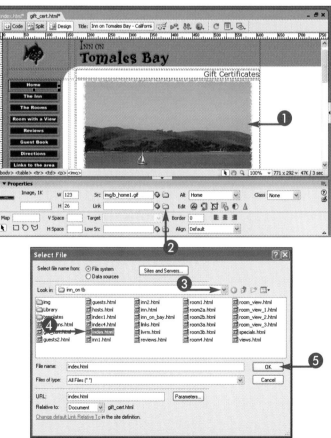

The Select File dialog box appears.

3. Click here and select the folder that contains the destination page.

4. Click the HTML file to which you want to link.

5. Click **OK**.

Your image becomes a link.

● Dreamweaver automatically inserts the filename and path to the linked page.

● You can test the link by previewing your page in a Web browser.

Note: To preview a page in a Web browser, see Chapter 2.

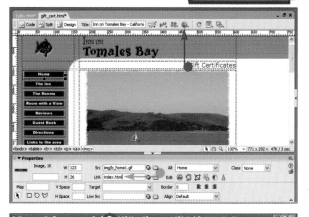

REMOVE A LINK FROM AN IMAGE

1 Click a linked image.

2 Click **Modify**.

3 Click **Remove Link**.

Dreamweaver removes the link.

How do I create a navigation bar for my Web page?

Many Web sites include sets of images that act as link buttons on the top, side, or bottom of each page. These button images allow viewers to navigate through the pages of the Web site. You can create these button images by using an image-editing program such as Adobe Photoshop or Macromedia Fireworks, and then use Dreamweaver to insert them into the page and create the links.

How will visitors to my Web site know to click an image?

When a visitor rolls a cursor over an image that serves as a link, their cursor turns into a hand. You can make it clearer which images are linked by putting links in context with other content, and by grouping links to let visitors know that images are clickable.

Create a Jump Link within a Page

You can create a link to other content on the same page. Same-page links, often called *jump links* or *anchor links*, are commonly used on long pages when you want to provide an easy way to navigate to relevant information lower on the page.

You create a jump link by first placing a named anchor where you want the link to go to and then linking from the text or image to the named anchor point.

Create a Jump Link within a Page

1. Position the mouse ⌖ where you want to insert the named anchor.

2. Click **Insert**.

3. Click **Named Anchor**.

The Named Anchor dialog box appears.

4. Type a name for the anchor.

5. Click **OK**.

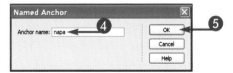

● An anchor appears in the Document window.

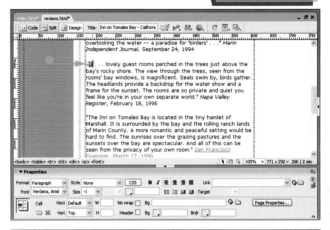

6 Click and drag to select the text that you want to link to the anchor.

7 In the Link field in the Properties inspector, type a pound sign (#), followed by the name of the anchor.

Dreamweaver links the selected text to the named anchor.

● You can test the link by previewing the file in a Web browser.

Note: *To preview a Web page in a Web browser, see Chapter 2.*

Why would you create a jump link to something on the same page?

Web designers often use jump links, or same-page hyperlinks, to make it easier to find text that appears lower on a page. For example, these links are frequently used as Back to Top links that bring you to the beginning of a page when you click a link lower on the page. If you have a Web page that is a glossary, same-page links allow you to link to different parts of the glossary from a link menu at the top of the page. A Frequently Asked Questions (FAQ) page is another example of when to use same-page links, because you can list all of your questions at the top of the page to make it easier to find the answers.

Create a Link to Another File Type

Links do not have to lead just to other Web pages. You can also link to other file types, such as image files, word processing documents, PDF files, and multimedia files. Many of these files require their own players, but as long as your visitor has the required program, the file opens automatically when the user clicks the link.

Create a Link to Another File Type

1 Click and drag to select the text that you want to turn into a link.

2 Click the **Link** 🖾 in the Properties inspector.

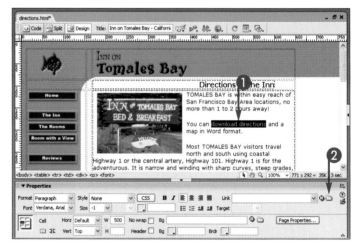

The Select File dialog box appears.

3 Click here and select the folder that contains the destination file.

4 Click the file to which you want to link.

5 Click **OK**.

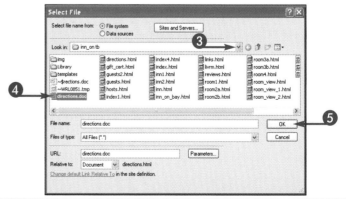

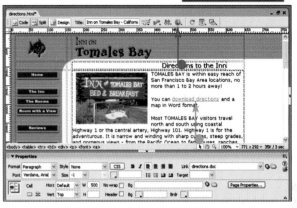

● The new link appears in a color and underlined.

Note: *Links are not clickable in the Document window.*

● You can test the link by previewing the file in a Web browser.

Note: *To preview a page in a Web browser, see Chapter 2.*

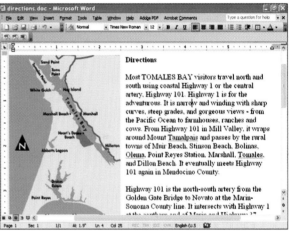

When you click the link in a Web browser, the linked file opens.

In this example, a Word document opens in Microsoft Word.

 TIP

How do users see files that are not HTML documents?

What users see when they click links to other types of files depends on how they have configured their Web browser and what applications they have installed on their computer. For example, if you link to a QuickTime movie (which has a .mov file extension), your visitors need to have a player that can display QuickTime movies. It is always good practice to include a link to the player for any special file type, to make it easy for users to find and download it if they choose.

Create an Image Map

You can link different areas of an image to different pages with an image map. First, you define areas of the image, called hotspots, using Dreamweaver's image-mapping tools, and then you turn them into links.

Create an Image Map

① Click an image.

② Type a name for the image map.

Note: You cannot use spaces or special characters in an image map name.

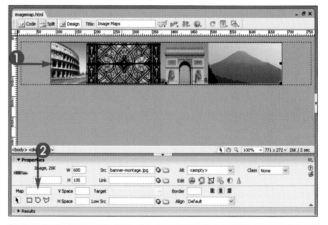

The name appears in the map field.

③ Click a drawing tool.

You can create rectangular shapes with the ▢ tool, oval shapes with the ◯ tool, and irregular shapes with the ▽ tool.

④ Draw an area on the image using the tool that you selected.

You can repeat Steps **3** to **8** to create as many hotspots as you want.

To delete a hotspot, select it, and then press Delete .

⑤ Click the **Map** ▢.

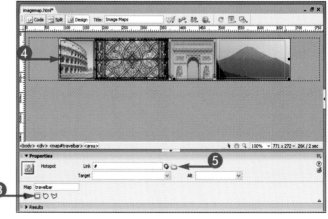

The Select File dialog box appears.

6 Click here and select the folder that contains the destination file.

7 Click the file to which you want to link.

8 Click **OK**.

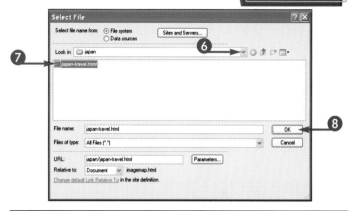

● The area defined by the selected shape links to the selected file. In this example, the image of the mountain links to a page about Japanese travel.

You can repeat Steps **3** to **8** to add other linked areas to your image.

The image-map shapes do not appear when you open the page in a Web browser.

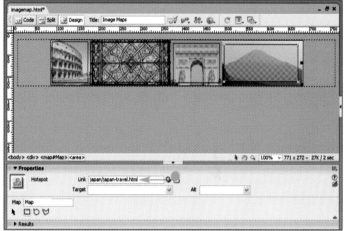

Can image maps be used for geographical maps that link to multiple locations?

An interactive geographical map, such as a map of Latin America, is a common place to see hotspots in action. You can create one by adding a graphic image of a map to your Web page and then defining a hotspot over each location to which you want to link. Use the Polygon tool () to draw around boundaries that do not follow a square shape. Finally, assign a different link to each hotspot.

Create a Link Using the Insert Menu

Dreamweaver provides multiple options for creating links. For example, you can create links quickly and easily using either the Properties inspector or the Insert menu.

Your Web pages only display in the Files panel if you have set up your site in Dreamweaver, an important first step that is covered in Chapter 2.

Create a Link Using the Insert Menu

Note: Arrange your workspace so that both the Document window and Files panel are visible for this task.

1 Click and drag to select the text that you want to turn into a link.

2 Click **Insert**.

3 Click **Make Link**.

The Select File dialog box appears.

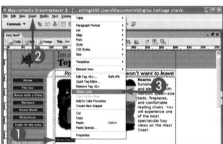

4 Click here and select the folder that contains the page to which you want to link.

5 Click the file name.

6 Click **OK**.

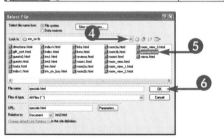

● The new link appears in color and underlined.

● The destination file displays in the Link field in the Properties inspector.

You can create a link that when clicked, opens a new browser window to display the destination page.

Opening a new browser window allows a user to keep the previous Web page open.

Open a Linked Page in a New Browser Window

① Click and drag to select the link that you want to open in a new browser window.

② Click the **Target** ⊡.

③ Click **_blank**.

④ Click 🔲 to preview the page in a Web browser.

Note: To preview a page in a Web browser, see Chapter 2.

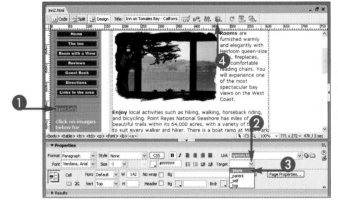

⑤ Click the link.

The link destination appears in a new browser window.

Create an E-Mail Link

You can create an e-mail link in your Web page. When a user clicks the link, it launches an e-mail program on the user's computer, creates a message, and inserts the e-mail address into the Address field.

Create an E-Mail Link

① Click to select the text or image that you want to turn into an e-mail link.

② Click **Insert**.

③ Click **Email Link**.

The Email Link dialog box appears, with the selected text in the Text field.

④ Type the e-mail address to which you want to link.

⑤ Click **OK**.

Dreamweaver creates your e-mail link.

To test the link, you can preview the page in a Web browser.

Check Links

You can automatically verify the links on a Web page. Using Dreamweaver's link-testing features, you can also receive a report that lists any links that are broken.

There are many ways in which links can become broken. Dreamweaver makes it easy to find and fix them.

Check Links

① Click **File**.

② Click **Check Page**.

③ Click **Check Links**.

● Dreamweaver checks the local links and lists any broken links that it finds in the Results panel.

Note: Dreamweaver cannot verify links to Web pages on external sites.

● You can edit a broken destination or image file by selecting it, and then using the Browse 📁 to locate the correct file.

You can also double-click the page to open it.

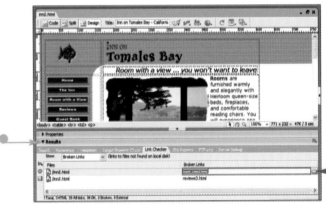

Change the Color of Links on a Page

You can change the color of the links on your Web page to make them match the visual style of the other text and images on your page.

Change the Color of Links on a Page

① Click **Modify**.

② Click **Page Properties**.

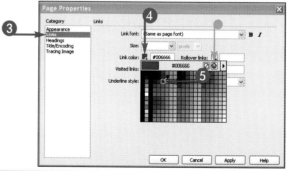

The Page Properties dialog box appears.

③ Click **Links**.

④ Click the **Link color** 🔲 (⟨ changes to 🖉).

⑤ Click a color from the menu using the 🖉 tool.

● You can click the **System Color Picker** (🔘) to select a custom color, or to specify no color.

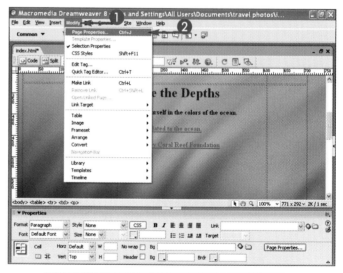

The color menu closes.

6 Click and select the colors for Visited links, Rollover links, and Active links.

This example defines the links with a hex number, but you can specify common colors on your Web page with their names. For example, you can specify the colors red or blue, instead of choosing the colors from the color menu.

Note: To change the color of links, see Chapter 5.

7 Click **OK**.

When you preview the page in a Web browser, the links display in the specified color.

Note: To preview a page in a Web browser, see Chapter 2.

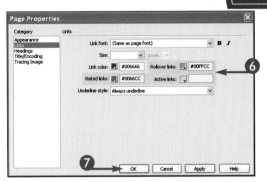

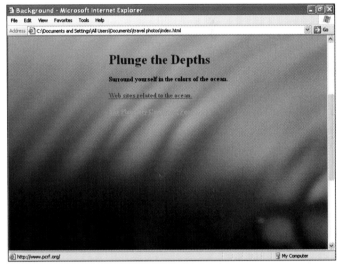

TIPS

What color will my links be if I do not choose colors for them?

Blue is the default link color in the Dreamweaver Document window. What viewers see when the page opens in a Web browser depends on their browser settings. By default, most Web browsers display unvisited links as blue, visited links as purple, and active links as red.

How can I override the link colors that I set?

Sometimes you may need to change the color of a linked word to something other than the set link color of a page — if it is set against a different background color or you want it to stand out better, for example. Select the text and use the Font in the Properties inspector to select a color. Once changed, the text always appears in that color, even after it is visited.

Using Tables to Design a Web Page

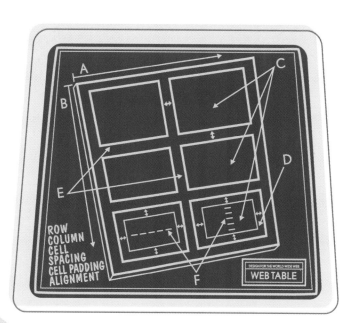

Tables enable you to arrange text, images, and other elements on your Web pages, and to create complex designs, even within the constraints of HTML. This chapter shows you how to create and format tables.

Insert a Table into a Web Page

You can use tables to organize and design pages that contain financial data, text, images, and multimedia. Dreamweaver's layout features allow you to create simple tables for tabular data or complex tables to create sophisticated layouts and designs.

Insert a Table into a Web Page

① Position the mouse ⟨ where you want to insert a table.

By default, the cursor snaps to the left margin. However, you can insert tables between existing elements on a page, and you can control table alignment.

② Click **Insert**.

③ Click **Table**.

The Table dialog box appears.

④ Type the number of rows and columns that you want in your table.

⑤ Type the width of your table.

You can set the width in pixels, or as a percentage of the page, by clicking ⊡ and selecting your choice of measurements.

⑥ Type a border thickness in pixels.

⑦ Click **OK**.

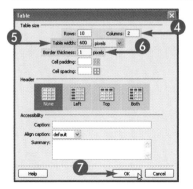

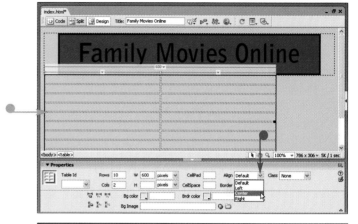

- An empty table appears, aligned to the left by default.
- You can click here and select a different alignment.

TURN OFF TABLE BORDERS

1 Click ☑.

2 Click **Select Table**.

3 Type the number **0** in the Border field.

4 Press Enter (Return).

When you view the page in a Web browser, the dashed table border disappears.

TIPS

How do I change the appearance of the content inside my table?

You can specify the size, style, and color of text inside a table in the same way that you format text on a Web page. Likewise, you can control the appearance of an image inside a table in the same way that you can control it outside a table. For more on formatting text, see Chapter 5, and for more on images, see Chapter 7.

Why would I turn off table borders?

Table borders can help to define the edges of a table and organize columnar data, such as a financial report. However, if you want to use a table to arrange photos and text within the design of your page, then you can have a cleaner layout if you set the border to zero so that it becomes invisible. Because most users do not want a border, Dreamweaver's default setting is zero. You can set it to one pixel for a slim border, or try five or ten if you want a thick border.

Insert Content into a Table

You can fill the cells of your table with the same content that you would insert on a Web page. This content can include text, images, multimedia files, form elements, and other tables.

Insert Content into a Table

INSERT TEXT

1 Click to place your mouse ⌖ inside a table cell.

2 Type text into the cell.

Note: To format your text, see Chapter 5.

INSERT AN IMAGE

1 Click inside a table cell.

2 Click **Image** (⊞).

The Select Image Source dialog box appears.

3 Click here and select the folder that contains your image.

4 Click an image file.

5 Click **OK**.

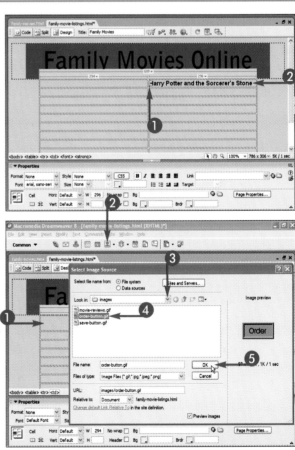

- The image appears in the table cell.

- If the image is larger than the cell, the cell expands to accommodate the image.

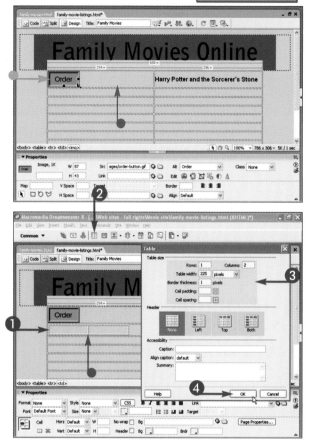

INSERT A TABLE WITHIN A TABLE

1 Click inside a table cell.

2 Click **Table** (▦).

The Table dialog box appears.

3 Type values in the fields to define the characteristics of the table.

4 Click **OK**.

- The new table appears within the table cell.

TIP

How can I add captions to images on my Web page?

The best way to add a caption to the top, bottom, or side of an image is by creating a two-celled table. Place the image in one cell and the caption in the other. You can then adjust the size and alignment of the table to position the captioned image within the rest of the content on your Web page.

Change the Background of a Table

You can change the background of a table, or only change the background of a cell, a row, or a column. This is a great way to add a design element or to call attention to a section of a table. Just like the background of a Web page, you can change the background color of a table, or fill the background of a table with an image. For more on Web page backgrounds, see Chapter 7.

Change the Background of a Table

① Click to select a table or individual cell, or click and drag to select a row or column of cells.

② Click the **Background** ▢ to open the color menu (🖑 changes to 🖉).

③ Click a color.

● You can click the **System Color Picker** (🔘) to select a custom color.

● You can delete the contents of the color field to specify no color.

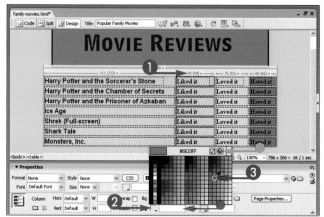

● The color fills the background of the selected cells.

● You can also type a color name or a color code into the Color field.

Note: To change the font color of a Web page, see Chapter 5.

ADD A BACKGROUND IMAGE TO A TABLE

1️⃣ Click a corner to select a table or cell, or click and drag to select multiple cells.

2️⃣ Click the **Background Image** 🖼 in the Properties inspector.

The Select Image Source dialog box appears.

3️⃣ Click here and select the folder that contains your image.

4️⃣ Click an image file.

5️⃣ Click **OK**.

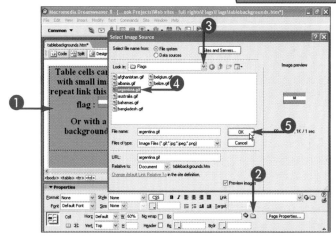

● The table or cell background fills with the image.

If the cell space is greater than the image size, then the image tiles fill the available area.

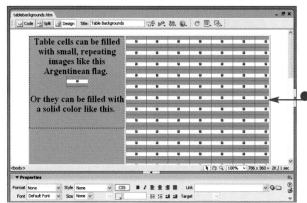

TIP

How can I change the background of a table cell?

Click inside a cell and then specify the background color using the Background Color 🔲, or insert a background image by clicking 🖼 and selecting an image from the Image Source dialog box. You can give each cell a different background or use one color to create an appearance of a solid area. You can also fill a cell with one large image in the background. You can then add text and other elements over the background.

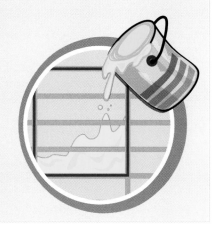

Change the Cell Padding in a Table

You can change the cell padding to add space between a table's content and its borders.

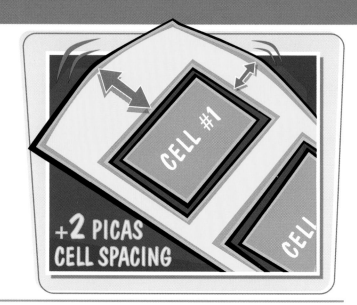

Change the Cell Padding in a Table

1 Click the top left corner of the table to select it.

2 In the CellPad field in the Properties inspector, type the amount of padding in pixels.

3 Press **Enter** (**Return**).

● The space changes between the table content and the table borders.

Note: Adjusting the cell padding affects all of the cells in a table. You cannot adjust the padding of individual cells by using the CellPad field.

You can change cell spacing to adjust the distance that cells are from each other.

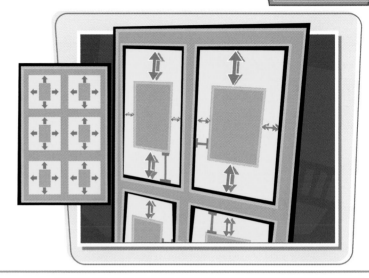

Change the Cell Spacing in a Table

1 Click the top left corner of the table to select it.

2 In the Cell Space field, type the amount of spacing in pixels.

● The cell spacing changes.

● You can change the width of the table or a column by clicking and dragging the cell borders.

Note: *Adjusting the cell spacing affects all of the cell borders in the table. You cannot adjust the spacing of individual cell borders by using the CellSpace field.*

Change the Alignment of a Table

You can change the alignment of a table and wrap text and other content around it, much like you would do with images and other elements.

① Click the top left corner of the table to select it.

② Click the Align ⬇.

③ Click an alignment option.

● The table aligns in the page.

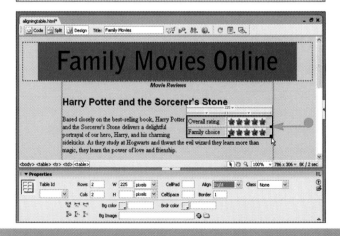

You can align the content in
your table cells horizontally and
vertically to center elements or
move them to the top or bottom
of a cell.

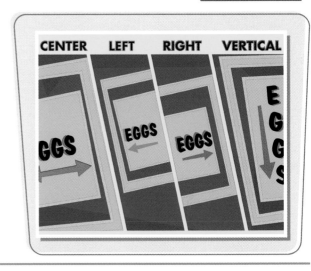

Change the Alignment of Cell Content

1 Click and drag to select the entire column.

You can press **Shift** + click, or click and drag, to
select multiple cells.

2 Click the Horizontal ⊡.

3 Click a horizontal alignment.

● The content aligns.

In this example, horizontal alignment was set to
center for four cells simultaneously.

Insert or Delete a Row or Column

You can insert cells into your table to add content or create space between elements. You can also delete rows or columns to remove them when they are not needed.

Insert a Row or Column

① Click the top left corner of the table to select it.

② Type the number of rows and columns that you want in the Properties inspector.

③ Press **Enter** (**Return**).

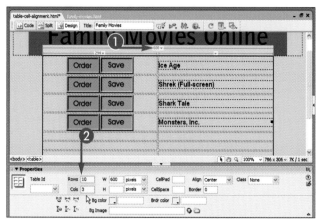

● Empty rows or columns appear in the table.

To add a row or column in the middle of a table, right-click inside an existing cell, click **Table**, and then click **Insert Row or Column** from the menu that appears. You can also click **Modify**, then click **Table**, and then click **Insert Row or Column**.

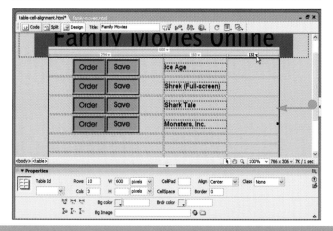

Delete a Row or Column

1 Press **Shift** + click, or click and drag, to select the cells that you want to delete.

2 Press **Delete**.

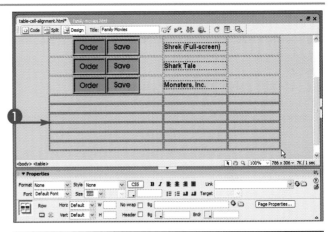

● The selected table cells disappear.

Note: The content of a cell is deleted when you delete a cell.

You can also delete cells by right-clicking inside the cells, then clicking **Table**, and then clicking **Delete Row** or **Delete Column** from the menu that appears. You can also click **Modify**, then click **Table**, and then click **Delete Row** or **Delete Column**.

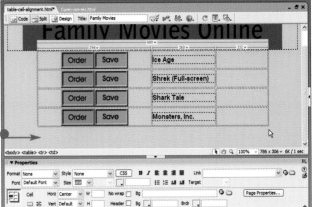

TIPS

What happens to the content of a deleted cell?
Dreamweaver does not warn you if the cells that you are deleting in a table contain content. This is because Dreamweaver assumes that you also want to delete the cell content. If you accidentally remove content when deleting rows or columns, you can click **Edit** and then click **Undo** to undo your last action.

How do I move content around a table?
You can move the contents of a table cell by clicking to select any image, text, or element in the cell and then dragging it out of the table or into another cell. You can also use copy and paste to move content from one cell to another, or to another part of a page.

Split or Merge Table Cells

You can create more elaborate page designs by splitting or merging cells in a table to create larger cells adjacent to smaller ones. You can then insert text, images and other content into the cells.

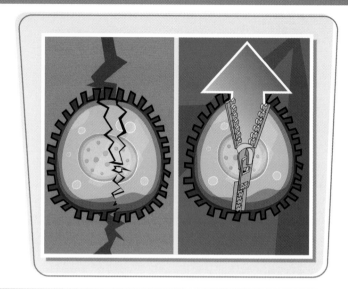

Split a Table Cell

1. Click to place your cursor in the cell that you want to split.

2. Click **Modify**.

3. Click **Table**.

4. Click **Split Cell**.

● You can also split a cell by clicking **Split Cell** (⬚) in the Properties inspector.

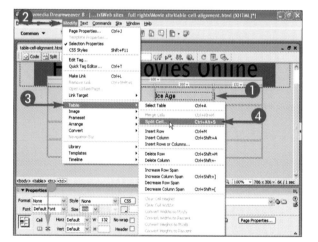

The Split Cell dialog box appears.

5. Click **Rows** or **Columns** to split the cell (○ changes to ◉).

6. Type the number of rows or columns.

7. Click **OK**.

● The table cell splits.

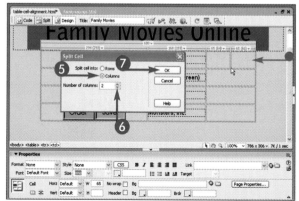

Merge Table Cells

① Click and drag to select the cells that you want to merge.

② Click **Modify**.

③ Click **Table**.

④ Click **Merge Cells**.

● You can also merge cells by clicking **Merge Cells** () in the Properties inspector.

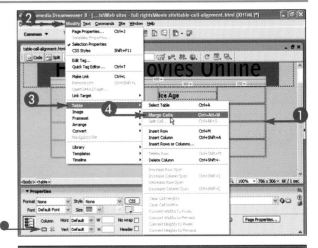

● The table cells merge.

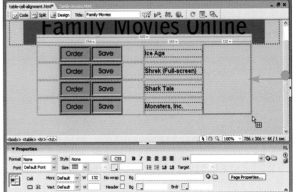

TIPS

Can I merge any combination of table cells?

No. The cells must have a rectangular arrangement. For example, you can merge all of the cells in a two-row-by-two-column table. However, you cannot select three cells that form an *L* shape and merge them into one cell.

Can I add as many cells as I want?

Yes, just make sure that your final table design displays well on a computer monitor. For example, although it is common to design Web pages that are long and require visitors to scroll down, it can be confusing to create overly wide pages that require scrolling right or left.

Change the Dimensions of a Cell

You can change the dimensions of individual table cells to better accommodate their content. As you enlarge and reduce cells, you can create more complex tables for more precise design control.

Change the Dimensions of a Cell

1 Click to select the edge of a cell and drag to adjust the size.

● You can also enter a size in the Properties inspector.

You can also specify a percentage of the table size instead of specifying pixels. For example, you can type **25** percent in the width or height box.

2 Press Enter (Return).

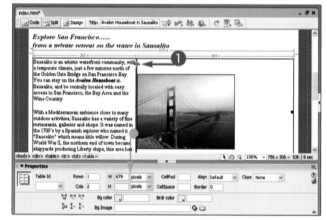

● The cell and its contents readjust to its new dimensions.

Note: Cell dimensions may be constrained by content. For example, Dreamweaver cannot shrink a cell smaller than the size of the content that it contains.

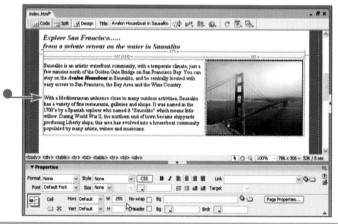

You can change the dimensions of your entire table. This is a good technique for ensuring that your content fits well within your Web page.

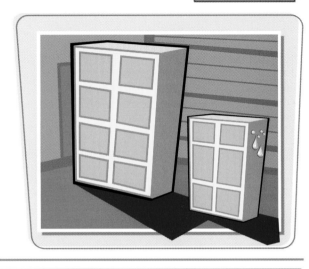

Change the Dimensions of a Table

1. Click the top left corner of the table to select it.

2. Type a width and height.

3. Click here and select the width setting in pixels, or a percentage of the screen.

4. Press **Enter** (**Return**).

● The table readjusts to its new dimensions.

Note: *Table dimensions may be constrained by content. For example, Dreamweaver cannot shrink a table smaller than the size of the content that it contains.*

If a height or width is not specified, the table automatically adjusts to fit the space that is available on the user's screen.

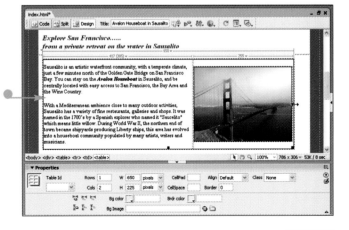

Create a Layout Table

You can create tables to better control the design of a Web page. Dreamweaver makes this easier with its table layout features, which allow you to click and drag to draw tables and cells anywhere on a page.

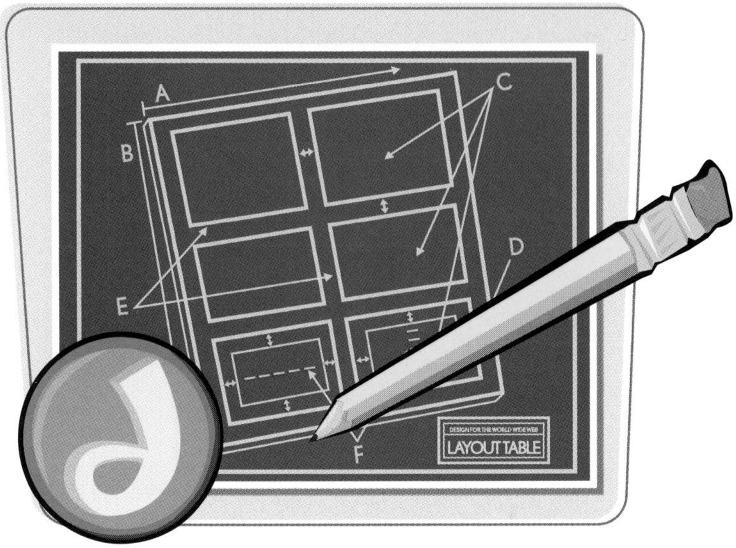

Create a Layout Table

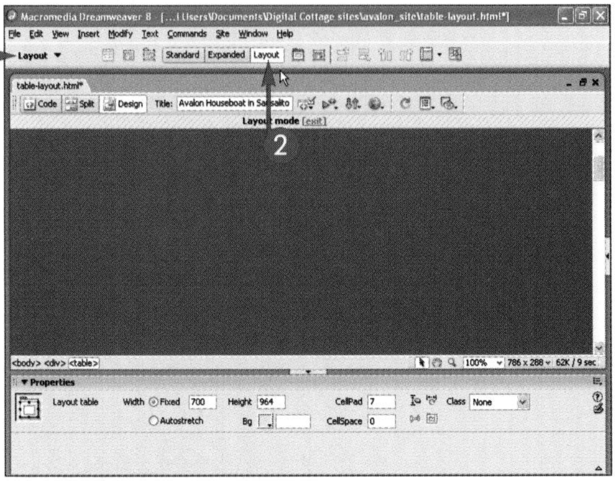

1. Click here and select **Layout** from the Insert bar.

   The Layout options appear in the Insert bar.

2. Click **Layout**.

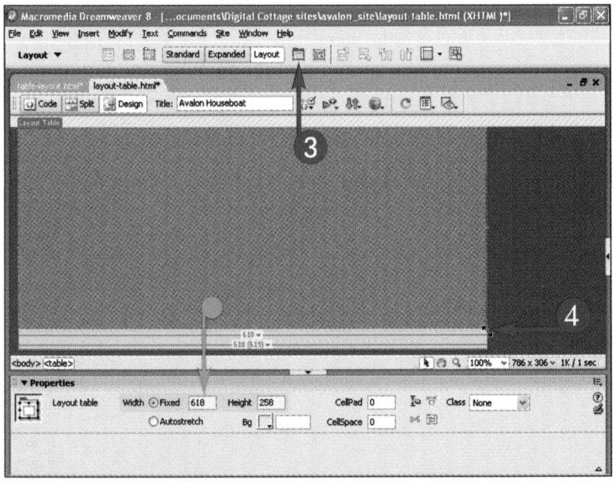

3. Click **Layout Table** (▣) (↖ changes to +).
4. Click and drag the mouse + to create a table.

   The outline of a table appears.

- You can specify the exact size of the table in the Properties inspector.

5 Click **Layout Cell** (image) (↳ changes to ↳).

6 Click and drag inside the table to create a Layout Cell.

The attributes of the cell appear in the Properties inspector.

● You can adjust the size and position of a cell by clicking and dragging its edge or by clicking the center of the border where the dots appear.

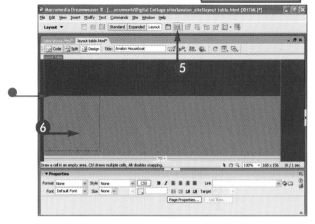

7 Click to position your mouse ↳ in the cell, and add content as you would anywhere else on the page.

Note: To insert content, see the section "Insert Content into a Table" in this chapter.

● You can click the **Common** option in the Insert bar to access the Insert Image (image) and other buttons.

Although you can insert content in Layout view in the same way as you do in Standard view, it is easier to tab around a table in Standard view.

TIPS

What can I do to draw my layout table cells more precisely?

It is easy, you just click and drag to create tables and cells in Layout view anywhere on the page. In Standard Layout view, you have to merge and split cells to try to position a cell, which makes it much harder to be precise. Click **Layout** on the Insert Layout bar to use Layout view.

Can I create a cell anywhere I want?

In Layout view, you can draw table cells anywhere inside a table. Simply click and drag to create a cell. Dreamweaver fills in any necessary cells as it creates a complex table in the background, with spacers to control the exact positioning of elements in your page design.

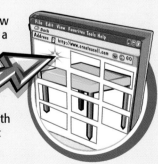

Rearrange a Table

In Layout or Standard view, you can easily change the size of the cells in a table. You can also click and drag to move content from one cell in a table to another cell or table.

MOVE THE CONTENTS OF A CELL OR TABLE

① Click to select an element, such as an image.

② Click and drag the content to the desired location.

Note: Do not click and drag a handle, or you risk resizing the element or the table cell.

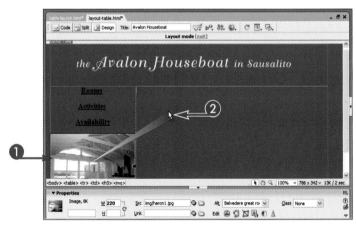

● The content appears in the new location.

Undefined cells in the table adjust their sizes to make room for the content of the cell.

CHANGE THE SIZE OF A TABLE OR A CELL

① Click the edge of the table or an individual cell
(⬧ changes to ↔).

② Click and drag a side or corner handle to the
desired size.

● The table or cell resizes.

Note: You cannot overlap cells in a table.

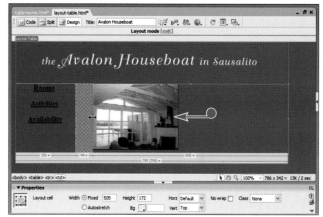

How do I delete a cell in Layout view?
Click the edge of the
cell to select it and then
press Delete.
Dreamweaver replaces
the space with gray,
non-editable cells that it
uses as space holders to
maintain the placement
of other cells.

How do I delete a table in Layout view?
Click ⬇ and click **Select Table** to select an entire
table, and then press
Delete. If you decide that
you want to change the
design, then you may find
that it is easier to delete a
table and start over than to
make adjustments to an
existing one.

Adjust the Width of a Table

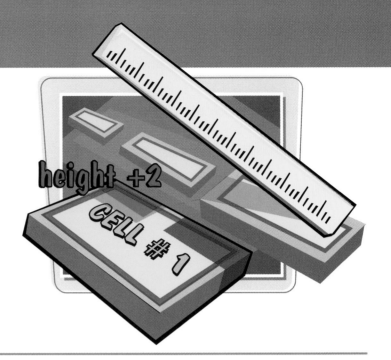

You can specify the size of a table using percentage instead of pixels. As a result, the table automatically adjusts to fit a user's browser window size.

When you define a table size as a percentage, it adjusts to fill that percentage of a user's browser window.

Adjust the Width of a Table

CREATE A FIXED-WIDTH COLUMN

① Click **Layout** in the Layout bar to change to Layout view.

② Click at the top or bottom of a column.

③ Click **Add Spacer Image** from the menu that appears.

If your site lacks a spacer image file that it can reference, a dialog box appears asking whether you want to create one. Click **OK**.

● A spacer image is inserted into the cell to maintain a fixed width.

Spacer images are transparent so that they do not appear in the display.

● A bar appears at the bottom of the cell containing the spacer image, indicating the size of the image.

CREATE AN AUTOSTRETCH COLUMN

1 Click at the top or bottom of a column.

2 Click **Make Column Autostretch** from the menu that appears.

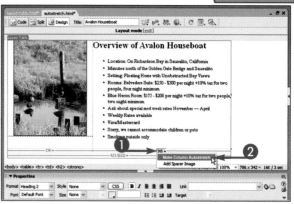

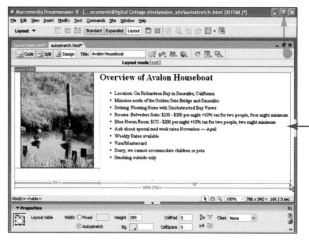

● Dreamweaver sets the column size to automatically adjust to fill up any available space on the screen.

● To see the autostretch effects in your browser window, resize the window.

Note: To preview a page in a Web browser, see Chapter 2.

TIPS

What is a spacer image?

A *spacer image* is a transparent GIF image file that is used as a filler to invisibly control spacing on a Web page. Essentially, you insert a spacer image into a table cell and then use the height and width attributes to control the size. The invisible image ensures that blank spaces on your page remain consistent. This is important because browsers sometimes display elements closer together if there is no text or image to prevent tightening up the design.

How do you make a spacer image?

Although Dreamweaver automatically creates spacer images, you can create your own in an image-editing program, such as Adobe Photoshop. Create a new image and set the background color to transparent. Save it as a GIF file in your Web site. An ideal size for a spacer image is 10 x 10 pixels; however, it can be any size. You can resize it in Dreamweaver to fit the space that you want to fill.

SAVE AS
spacer.gif

CHAPTER 9

Creating Pages with Frames

You can divide the display area of a Web browser into multiple panes by creating frames. Frames offer another way to organize information by splitting up your pages. For example, you can keep linked content visible in one frame and target it to open in a different frame within the same browser window.

Introduction to Frames

Frames enable you to divide your Web page into multiple sections and display different content in each frame.

A common use of frames is to place a list of navigation links in one frame, and have the links open their destination pages in a larger content frame.

Set Up a Frame

You can create a framed Web site in Dreamweaver by dividing the Document window horizontally or vertically one or more times. Each frame is composed of a different Web page that you can link independently. All pages in a frameset are described in a *frameset page*, and you must save them separately.

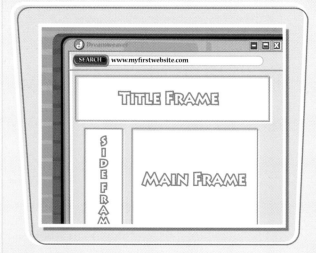

How Frames Work

Frames on a page operate independently of one another. As you scroll through the content of one frame, the content of the other frames remains fixed. You can create links in one frame that open in another frame.

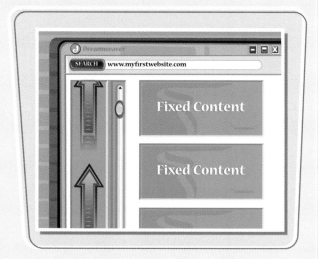

Insert a Predefined Frameset

You can easily create popular frame styles using the predefined framesets. You can access frame styles from the Frames tab in the Insert panel. They are also available from the Sample Framesets that are featured in the new opening screen in Dreamweaver, and in the New Page Window.

Insert a Predefined Frameset

① Click **File**.

② Click **New**.

The New Document dialog box appears.

③ Click a frameset.

④ Click **Create**.

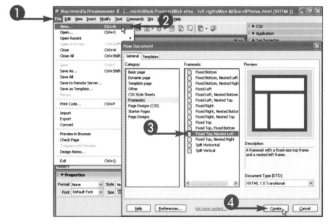

● Dreamweaver automatically creates all of the frames in the work area.

Scroll bars appear if the content extends outside of the frame borders.

● You can also click 🔲 and select a predefined frameset design from the Layout Insert bar.

Note: To add text, images, or other elements to a new frame, see Chapters 5 and 7.

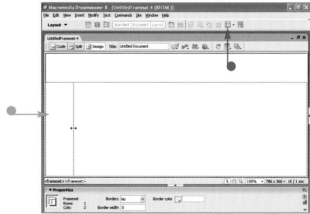

Save a Frameset

Saving your frameset requires you to save each of the individual pages that appear in the frames, as well as the frameset that defines how each frame appears.

You first need to save all of the individual documents before you can preview your work in a Web browser, or upload the frameset files to your Web site.

Save a Frameset

SAVE YOUR FRAMED PAGES

1. Click inside the frame that you want to save.

2. Click **File**.

3. Click **Save Frame**.

   The Save Frame command appears gray if the current frame is already saved.

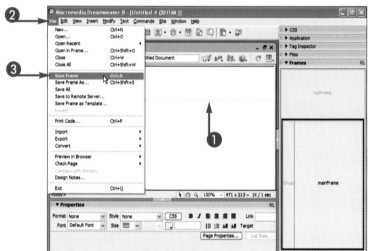

The Save As dialog box appears.

4. Click here and select the folder where you want to save the framed page.

5. Type a name for the page.

6. Click **Save**.

   Dreamweaver saves the page.

   Repeat Steps **1** to **6** to save other framed pages. You must save each page with a different file name.

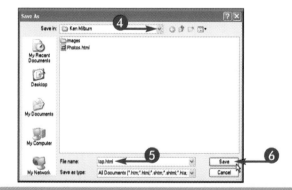

SAVE THE FRAMESET

1. Click anywhere on the frame border to select the entire frameset.

2. Click **File**.

3. Click **Save Frameset**.

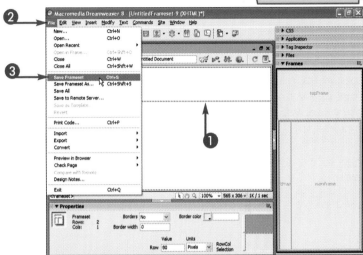

The Save As dialog box appears.

4. Click here and select the folder where you want to save the frames.

5. Type a name for the page.

6. Click **Save**.

Dreamweaver saves the frameset.

You can click **Save Frameset** or **Save All** in the File menu to save all of the files in a frameset.

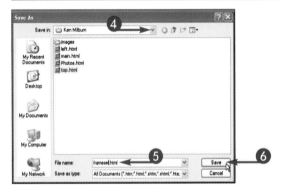

 TIPS

Is there a shortcut for saving all of the pages of my framed Web site?

Yes. You can click **File** and then click **Save Frameset**. This saves all of the framed pages and framesets that make up your Web site. Although this is definitely a time saver, you should take note of each file name so that you know what you have named each frame later. Otherwise, it can be tricky to identify them if you want to make changes.

What steps do I take if I want to change just one frame?

You can open any existing page into a frame area. Place your mouse in the frame that you want to change, click **File**, and then click **Open** to open an existing page. You can also click **File** and then click **New** to create a new page in the designated frame area.

Divide a Page into Frames

You can split a Document window vertically to create a frameset with left and right frames, or you can split it horizontally to create a frameset with top and bottom frames. You can also combine them to create more complex frames, or add frames to a predefined frameset.

Divide a Page into Frames

① Click **Modify**.

② Click **Frameset**.

③ Click a Split Frame command.

● The window splits into two frames. If content existed in the original page, then it shifts to one of the new frames.

Scroll bars appear if the content extends outside the frame borders.

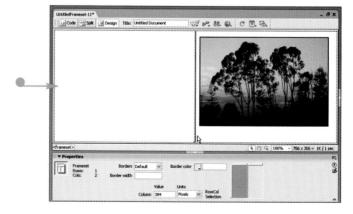

Create a Nested Frame

You can subdivide a frame of an existing frameset to create nested frames. With nested frames, you can organize the information in your site in a more complex way.

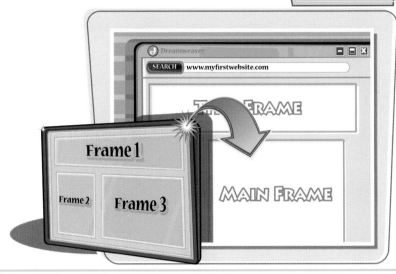

Create a Nested Frame

① Click inside the frame that you want to subdivide.

② Click **Modify**.

③ Click **Frameset**.

④ Click a Split Frame command.

● Dreamweaver splits the selected frame into two frames, thus creating a nested frame.

You can continue to split your frames into more frames.

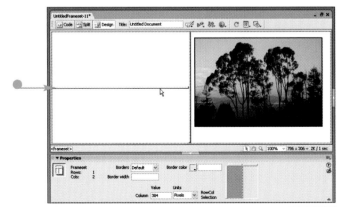

Change the Attributes of a Frame

You can change the dimensions of a frame to attractively and efficiently display the information inside it. You can also change scrolling and other options in the Properties inspector.

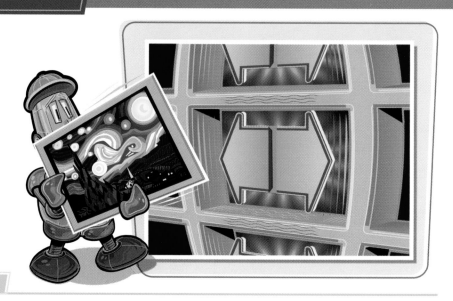

① Click a frame border to select the frame that you want to change.

② Type a column size.

③ Click here and select pixels, a percentage, or a relative value for the display area.

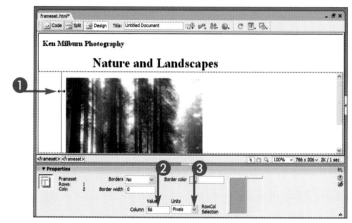

● The column widens.

● You can also click a frame border and drag it to the desired size (⟰ changes to ⟷).

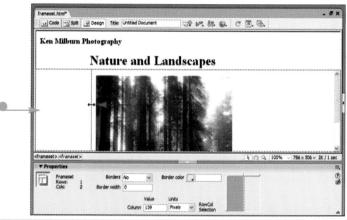

Change the Attributes of a Frame

① Click **Window**.

② Click **Frames**.

● The Frames Advanced Layout panel opens.

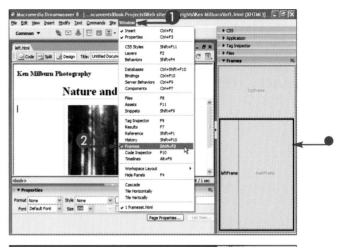

③ In the Frames panel, click a frame to select it.

④ Click here and select a Scroll attribute.

You can also adjust other attributes for borders and scrolling in the Properties inspector.

The frame changes.

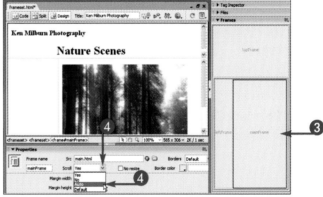

TIPS

Is there a shortcut for changing the dimensions of frames?

Yes. You can click and drag a frame border to quickly adjust the dimensions of a frame. The values in the Properties inspector change as you drag the frame border.

Why would I want to change scrolling options?

When the content in a frame exceeds the dimensions of a Web browser window, you should include a scroll bar so that visitors can view all of your content. If you set scrolling to Yes in the Properties inspector, then the scroll bar is always visible. If you set it to Auto, then a scroll bar appears only when needed.

Add Content
to a Frame

You can insert text, images, and other content into a frame just as you would in an unframed page. You can also link existing pages into a frameset.

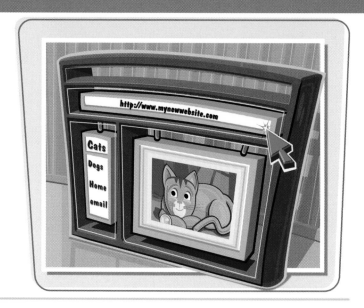

OPEN AN EXISTING FRAMESET

1 Click to position the mouse ℞ in the frame where you want to open an existing document.

2 Click **File**.

3 Click **Open in Frame**.

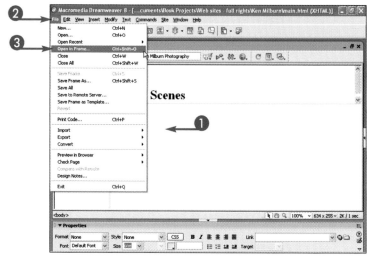

The Open dialog box appears.

4 Click here and select a folder.

5 Click the file that you want to open in the frame.

6 Click **Open**.

● The selected page appears in the frame area.

● If the content extends beyond the frame, then scroll bars automatically appear.

ADD NEW CONTENT TO A FRAME

1 Click inside the frame where you want to add text.

2 Type the text that you want to display.

● You can also add images, tables, or other elements by clicking the **Common** tab and then clicking **Insert Image** (🖼️) or **Insert Table** (▦) from the Insert panel.

Can I link a frame to a page on the Web?

Yes. You can link to an external Web-page address by using the Link field in the Properties inspector. However, unlike other pages, you must specify the target. To create targeted links, see "Create a Link to a Frame."

Can I add as much content as I want to a frame page?

Yes. A frame page is just like any other page. You can add as much text, images, and other content as you want. However, if you have a small frame, then you can have better design results by limiting the text within that frame page to fit the small space.

Delete a Frame

You can delete existing frames or create new frames in a frameset to change or expand a design.

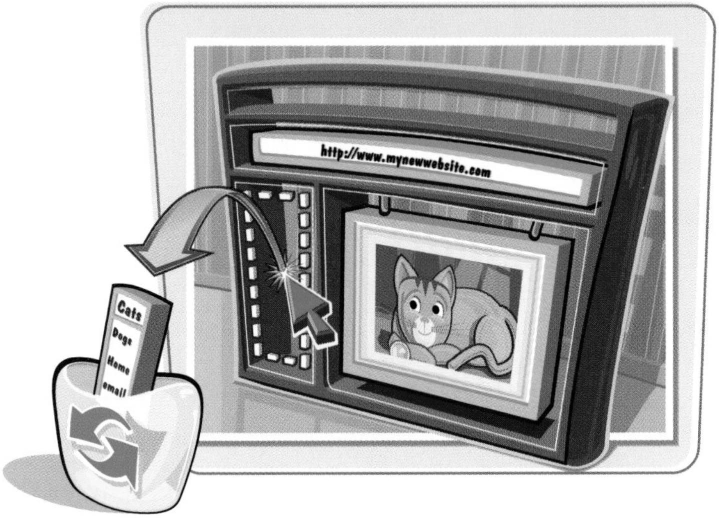

Delete a Frame

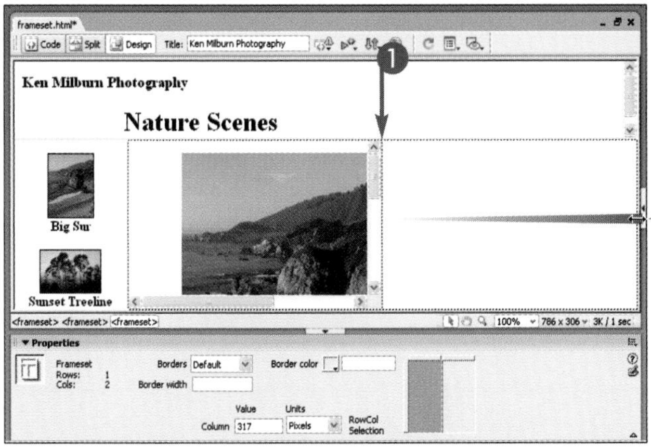

1 Position the mouse on the border of the frame that you want to delete (changes to ⟷).

2 Click and drag the border to the edge of the window.

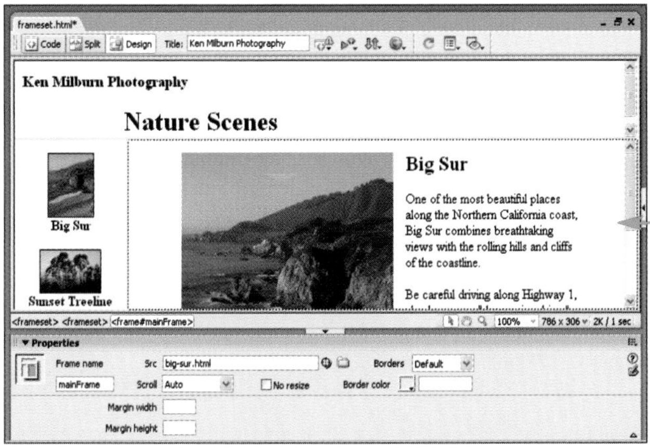

- Dreamweaver deletes the frame.

Before you can target links in one frame to open in another frame, you need to ensure that all of your frames have names. You use frame names to identify where the linked page should open in the frameset. Frame names are visible in the Frames panel.

This is Fred and Sarah, two good frames of mine.

Name a Frame

① Click to select the frame that you want to name in the Frames panel.

② Type a name for the frame.

③ Press **Enter** (**Return**).

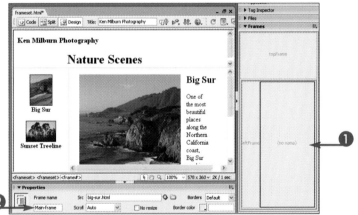

● The name of the frame appears in the Frames panel.

If the panel is not open, click **Window** and then click **Frames** to display it.

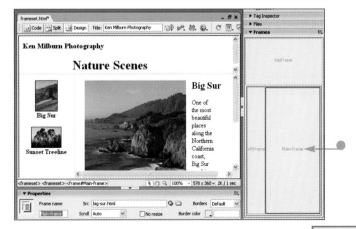

Create a Link to a Frame

You can create links in one frame that open a page in another frame. This is a common technique for navigation rows and other links that you want to continue to display when the linked page opens. For more information about creating links, see Chapter 8.

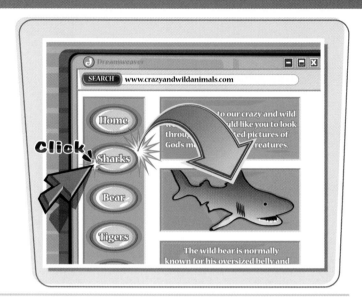

Create a Link to a Frame

① Click to select the text or image that you want to turn into a link.

② Click 🗁 in the Properties inspector.

The Select File dialog box opens.

③ Click here and select the folder containing the page to which you want to link.

④ Click the file.

⑤ Click **OK**.

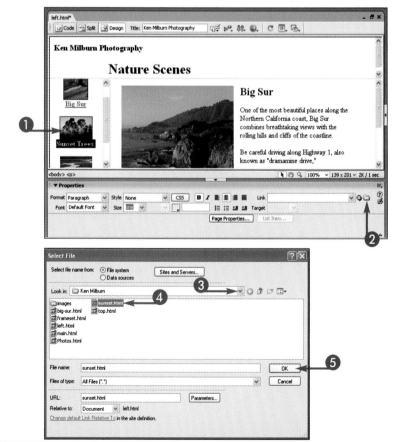

6 Click the **Target** ⊡.

7 Click to select the name of the frame where you want the target file to open.

Dreamweaver automatically names frames when they are created. Frame names are visible in the Frames panel.

8 Click ▣ to preview the page in a Web browser.

Note: To preview a page in a Web browser, see Chapter 2.

When you open the framed page in a Web browser and click the link, the destination page opens inside the targeted frame.

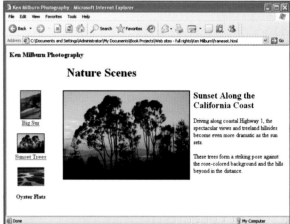

How do I create a link that opens a new page, outside of the frameset?

When you target a link, you can click **_top** from the Link drop-down menu in the Properties inspector, instead of a frame name, to open the linked page in its own new browser window. This action takes the user out of the frameset, and is especially recommended when linking to another Web site.

Can I target a link to another Web site?

Yes. You can create a link to another Web site from a framed page by entering the URL in the Link field in the Properties inspector. However, use this feature with care. Many Web site owners consider it bad form to display their Web pages within the frames on your Web site. Also, framing other Web sites can be confusing to visitors.

Format
Frame Borders

You can modify the appearance of your frame borders to make them complement your design. One way is to specify the color and width of your borders. You can also turn them off so that they are not visible.

SET BORDER SHADING, COLOR, AND WIDTH

① Click the corner of an outside frame border to select the entire frameset.

② Click here and select **Yes** or **Default** to turn on borders.

③ Type a border width in pixels.

④ Click the **Border color** ☐ (⬚ changes to 🖋).

⑤ Click a color.

● The frame border appears at the specified settings.

You can override the settings either at the frameset level or at the individual frame level if you want to change the settings to alter the border size or color.

You can also press and hold Alt (Option) and click inside a frame to select it. Then you can specify formatting in the Properties inspector.

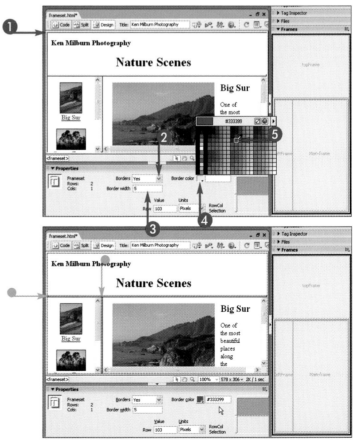

166

TURN OFF BORDERS

1 Click the corner of an outside frame border to select the entire frameset.

2 Click the **Borders** ⊡.

3 Click **No**.

4 Click ⬚ to preview the page in a Web browser.

Note: To preview a page in a Web browser, see Chapter 2.

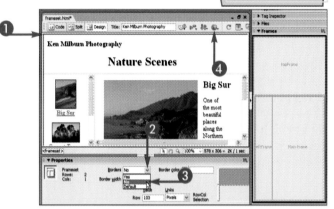

● The frame border does not display.

Links open in the targeted frame, even with borders turned off.

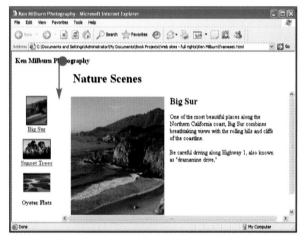

Why would I want to make my frame borders invisible?

Turning borders off can disguise the fact that you are using frames in the first place. If you want to further disguise your frames, you can set the pages inside your frames to the same background color. To change background colors, see Chapter 6.

What if the frames do not look right in a Web browser when I preview them?

It is not uncommon for frames to display differently in a Web browser than in Dreamweaver. If you find that the content is not exactly where you want it, or there are other problems with your frames, then simply return to Dreamweaver, click and drag to adjust frame borders, and make any necessary adjustments to your content.

Control Scroll Bars in Frames

You can control whether or not scroll bars appear in your frames. Although hiding scroll bars enables you to have more control over the presentation of your Web site, it can also prevent some users from seeing your entire Web site content.

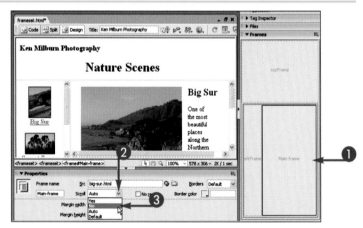

1 Click a frame in the Frames panel to select it.

2 Click the **Scroll** ⊡.

3 Click a Scroll setting.

You can click **Yes** to keep scroll bars on, click **No** to turn scroll bars off, or click **Auto** to keep scroll bars on when necessary. In most Web browsers, Default and Auto settings have the same result.

● The frame appears with the new setting.

In this example, scroll bars are turned off in the main frame. They remain on in the left frame so that viewers can access all of the navigation links in that frame by scrolling up and down.

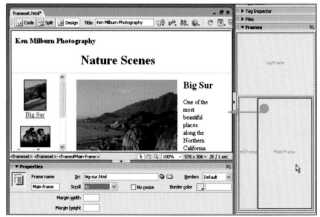

By default, most browsers allow
users to resize frames by clicking
and dragging frame borders.

**You can prevent users from resizing
the frames of a Web site. However,
depending on the size of their monitor,
you may make it impossible for them
to view all of your content.**

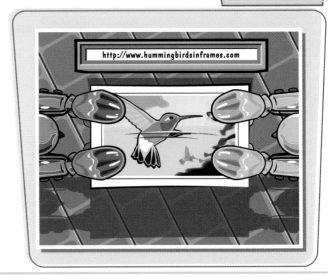

Control Resizing in Frames

① In the Frames panel, click a frame to select it.

② Click the **No resize** check box to remove the check
mark if one is visible (☑ changes to ☐).

③ Click 🖳 to preview the page in a Web browser.

Note: *To preview a page in a Web browser, see Chapter 2.*

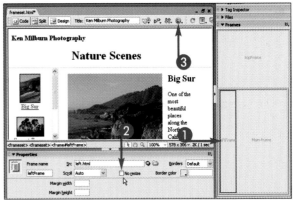

● The browser allows the user to resize the frame.

When you select the No Resize option, the browser
prevents the user from resizing the frame.

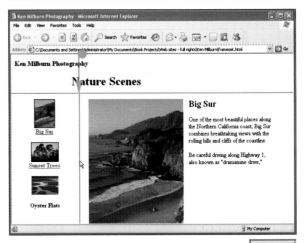

Creating
Web-Based Forms

You can allow your Web site visitors to send you information by creating forms on your Web pages. This chapter shows you how to create forms with different types of fields, buttons, and menus.

Introduction to Forms

You can add forms to your Web site to make it more interactive, thus allowing viewers to enter and submit information to you through your Web pages.

Forms work in conjunction with a program or script that processes the form information. Programmers generally create form scripts, and some scripts may be available through your service provider.

Create a Form

You can use Dreamweaver to construct a form by inserting text fields, pull-down menus, check boxes, and other interactive elements into your page. You can also enter the Web address of a form handler, or script, in Dreamweaver so that the information can be processed. Visitors to your Web page fill out the form and send the information to the script on your server by clicking a Submit button.

Process Form Information

Form handlers or *scripts* are programs that process the form information and execute an action, such as forwarding the information to an e-mail address or entering the contents of a form into a database. Although many ready-made form handlers are available for free on the Web, they generally require some customization. Your Web-hosting company may have forms available for you to use with your site. You can often find them by searching your hosting company's Web site or by calling tech support.

You can set up a form on your Web page by first creating a form container. The form container defines the area of the form where you place any text fields, menus, or other form elements. You associate the script or form handler by typing the name in the Properties inspector.

Define a Form Area

① Click where you want to insert your form.

② Click **Insert**.

③ Click **Form**.

④ Click **Form**.

You can also click the **Forms** item in the Insert Bar menu, and then click **Form** (▣).

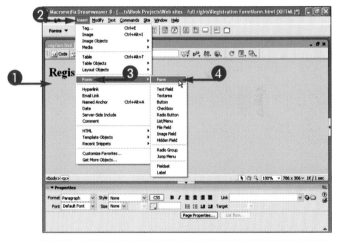

● A red, dashed box appears on the page, indicating that the form container is set up. To build the form, you can add form elements inside the red box.

⑤ Type the address of the form handler or script in the Action field.

You can get the address from the programmer who created your form script.

⑥ Click here and select **POST** or **GET**.

Your selection should be based on the command that is required by the script or form handler that you are using.

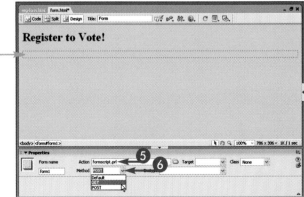

Add a Text Field to a Form

You can add a text field to enable viewers to submit text through your form. Text fields are probably the most common form element, enabling users to enter names, addresses, brief answers to questions, and other short pieces of text.

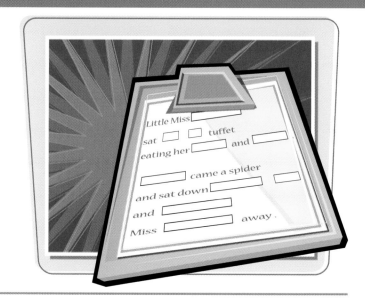

Add a Text Field to a Form

① Click inside the form container where you want to insert the text field.

② Click here and select **Forms**.

③ Click **Text Field** (☐) on the Forms bar.

An Input Tag Accessibility Attributes dialog box appears.

④ Type a label.

⑤ Select the accessibility attributes (○ changes to ●).

⑥ Click **OK**.

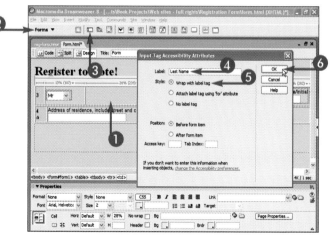

● A text field appears in your form with the text that you entered in the Input Tag Accessibility Attributes dialog box.

● Although the default Type option is Single line, you can click **Multi line** (○ changes to ●) if you want a text box with more than one line available for text.

● You can change the assigned name of the text field in the text field area.

⑦ Type an initial value for the text field if you want the text to appear in the text field box in the form.

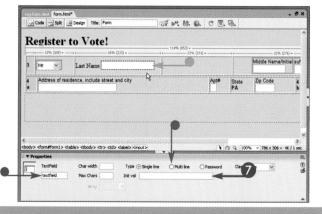

⑧ Type a character width to define the width of the text field.

⑨ Type a maximum number of characters to limit the amount of text that a user can enter.

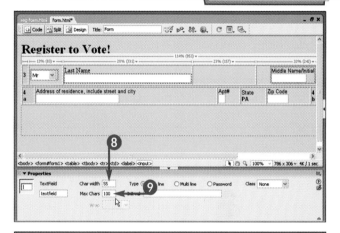

⑩ Double-click the text field and type to edit the label.

● You can apply formatting options in the Properties inspector.

Dreamweaver applies your specifications to the text field.

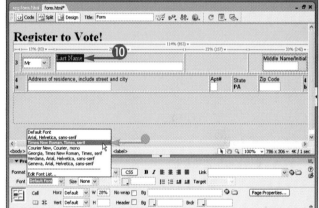

TIPS

Can I define the style of text that appears in the text field?

By default, the browser determines what style of text appears in form fields. It is not possible to format this type of text with plain HTML. You can use style sheets to manipulate the way the text in the form fields appears. However, keep in mind that only newer browsers support this formatting option. You can read more about style sheets in Chapter 12.

Can I create a text field with multiple lines?

Yes. When a text field has multiple lines, it is called a text area. You can insert a text area just as you insert a text field, by clicking the **Text Field** (▭) button in the Forms bar at the top of the screen.

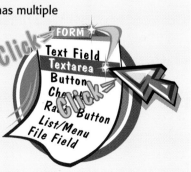

Add a Check Box to a Form

Check boxes enable you to present multiple options in a form and allow the user to select one, several, or none of the options.

Add a Check Box to a Form

① Click inside the form container where you want to insert the check box.

② Click here and select **Forms**.

③ Click **Check Box** (☑) on the Forms bar.

The Input Tag Accessibility Attributes dialog box appears.

④ Type a label.

⑤ Select the accessibility attributes that you want (◯ changes to ◉).

⑥ Click **OK**.

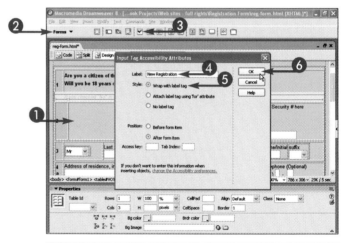

● The check box and label appear on the page.

⑦ Repeat Steps **2** to **5** until you have the number of check boxes that you want in your form.

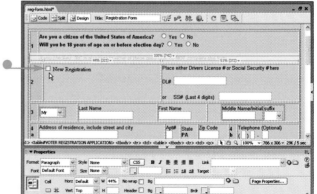

8 Click a check box (☐ changes to ☑).

9 Click to select an Initial state option
(○ changes to ⦿).

You should specify other attributes in the Properties inspector, such as the Checked value, based on the form handler or script that you are using.

10 Click to select the other check boxes in the group, one at a time, and specify attributes.

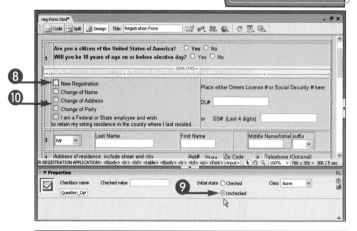

11 Click and drag to select a check box label.

12 Format the text using the Properties inspector.

Dreamweaver applies your formatting to the label.

TIPS

When should I use check boxes?

Check boxes are ideal when you want visitors to be able to select more than one option. Keep in mind that you may want to include the message, Check all that apply.

When should I use radio buttons?

When you want visitors to select only one option from a list of two or more, radio buttons are the best choice. You can set up your radio buttons so that it is not possible to select more than one option.

Add a Radio Button to a Form

You can allow visitors to select one of several options by adding a set of radio buttons to your form. With radio buttons, a user cannot select more than one option from a set.

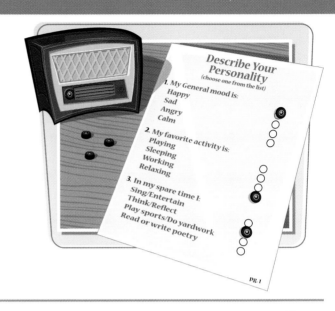

Add a Radio Button to a Form

1. Click inside the form container where you want to insert a radio button.

2. Click **Radio Button** (⊙) on the Forms bar.

   The Input Tag Accessibility Attributes dialog box appears.

3. Type a label.

4. Select the accessibility attributes that you want (◯ changes to ⊙).

5. Click **OK**.

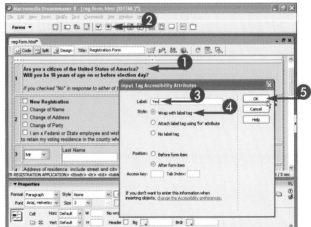

● A radio button and a label appear on the page.

6. Repeat Steps **2** to **5** until you have the number of radio buttons that you want in your form.

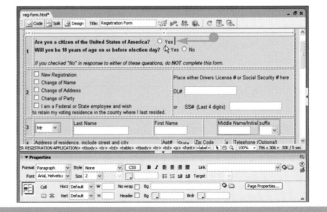

⑦ Click a radio button (◯).

⑧ Click to select an Initial state option
(◯ changes to ◉).

You should specify other attributes in the Properties inspector, such as the Checked value, based on the form handler or script that you are using.

⑨ Click to select the other radio buttons one at a time, and specify attributes for each radio button individually.

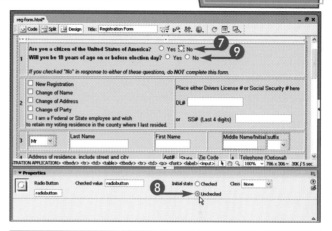

⑩ Click and drag to select radio button labels.

⑪ Format the text using the Properties inspector.

Dreamweaver applies your formatting to the label.

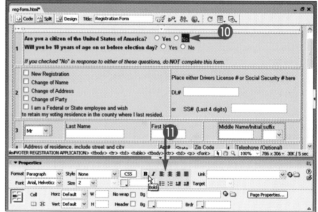

TIPS

What happens if I give each radio button in a set a different name?

If you do this, then a user can select more than one button in the set at a time, and after a button is selected, the user cannot deselect it. This defeats the purpose of radio buttons. If you want to enable your users to select more than one choice or to deselect a choice, then use check boxes (☑) instead of radio buttons (◉).

Are there alternatives to using check boxes or radio buttons?

Yes, there are alternatives such as menus and lists. Instead of using check boxes, you can use multi-select lists so that users can select more than one item from a list. You can replace a radio button with a menu that allows only one choice from a list.

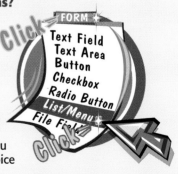

Add a Menu or List to a Form

Menus enable users to choose from a predefined list of choices. Similar to check boxes, users can choose one or more options from a menu or list.

Add a Menu or List to a Form

① Click inside the form container where you want a menu list.

② Click here and select **Forms**.

③ Click **Menu List** (▤) on the Forms bar menu.

The Input Tag Accessibility Attributes dialog box appears.

④ Type a label.

⑤ Select the accessibility attributes that you want (○ changes to ◉).

⑥ Click **OK**.

A blank menu appears in your form.

⑦ Click the menu to select it.

⑧ Click **List Values**.

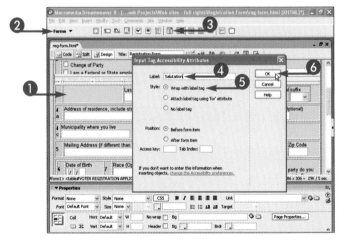

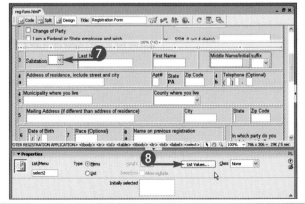

A List Values dialog box appears.

⑨ Type an Item Label and a Value for each menu item.

● You can click ⊞ or ⊟ to add or delete entries.

● You can select an item and click ▲ or ▼ to reposition the item in the list.

⑩ Click **OK** when you are done.

The entered values appear in the List box.

⑪ Click the item that you want to appear pre-selected when the page loads.

Dreamweaver applies your specifications to the menu.

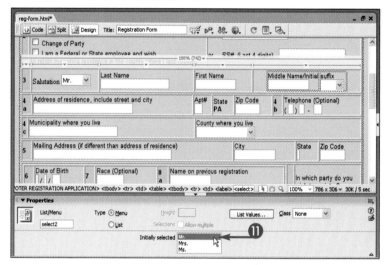

Add a Submit Button to a Form

At the end of your form, you need to add a Submit button. This enables users to send the information that they have entered into the form to the specified script or form handler.

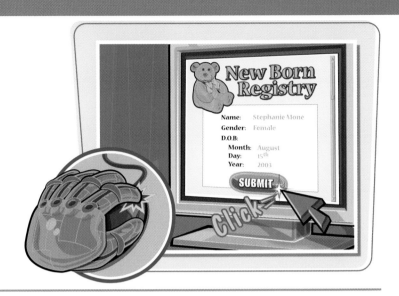

① Click inside the form container where you want to add the Submit button.

② Click here and select **Forms**.

③ Click **Create** (🔲) on the Forms bar.

The Input Tag Accessibility Attributes dialog box appears.

④ Type a label.

⑤ Select the accessibility attributes that you want (◯ changes to ◉).

⑥ Click **OK**.

A Submit button appears in the form.

⑦ Click the button to select it.

⑧ Type a Value for the button.

The text on the button changes from Submit to the value that you entered.

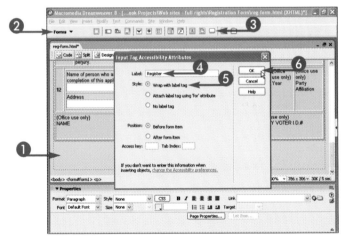

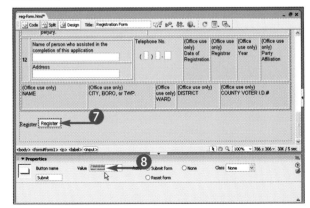

182

You can add a Reset button to a form to enable users to erase their form entries so that they can start over.

Add a Reset Button to a Form

1. Click inside the form container where you want to add the Reset button.

2. Click here and select **Forms**.

3. Click 🔲 on the Forms bar menu.

   The Input Tag Accessibility Attributes dialog box appears.

4. Type a label.

5. Select the accessibility attributes that you want (○ changes to ◉).

6. Click **OK**.

   A Reset button appears in the form.

7. Click the button to select it.

8. Click the **Reset form** radio button (○ changes to ◉).

● The Value automatically changes to Reset and the text on the button changes from Submit to Reset.

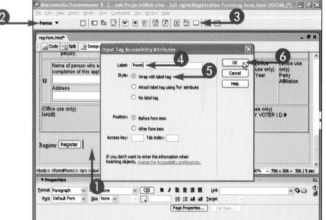

Using Library Items and Templates

You can save time by storing frequently used Web page elements and layouts as library items, and saving complete page designs as templates. This chapter shows you how to use these features to quickly create consistent page designs.

Introduction to Library Items and Templates

With library items and templates, you can avoid repetitive work by storing copies of page elements and layouts that you frequently use. You can access the library items and templates that you create through the Assets panel.

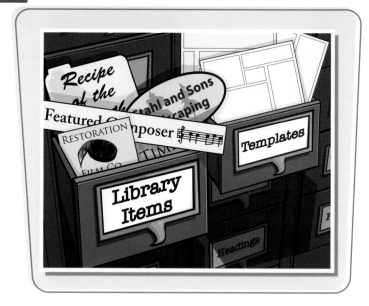

Library Items

You can define parts of your Web pages that are repeated in your Web site as library items. This saves you time because whenever you need a library item, you can just insert it from the Asset panel instead of recreating it. If you make changes to a library item, then Dreamweaver automatically updates all instances of the item across your Web site. Good candidates for library items include advertising banners, company slogans, navigation bars, and any other feature that appears many times across your Web site.

Templates

You can define entire Web pages as templates to save you time as you build new pages. Templates can also help you maintain a consistent page design throughout a Web site. After you make changes to a template, Dreamweaver automatically updates all of the pages in your Web site that were created from that template. When you use templates, you customize only the areas of the page that you want to change.

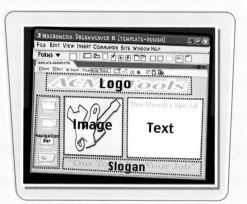

You can access the library and templates of a Web site by using commands in the Window menu. You can also access them through the Assets panel.

View Library Items and Templates

VIEW THE LIBRARY

1 Click **Window**.

2 Click **Assets**.

● The Assets panel opens.

3 Click **Library** (▣) to view the library items.

● The Library window opens in the Assets panel.

VIEW TEMPLATES

1 Click **Window**.

2 Click **Assets**.

● The Assets panel opens.

3 Click **Template** (▣) to view the templates.

● The Templates window opens in the Assets panel.

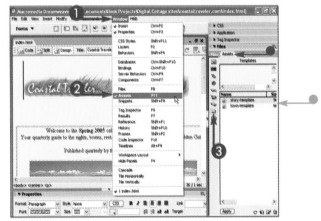

Create a Library Item

You can save text, links, images, and other elements as library items. Navigation rows are great examples of content that works well as a library item. This is because you can save a collection of images, text, and links that you can quickly insert into other pages without having to recreate them.

If you edit a library item, Dreamweaver automatically updates each instance of the item throughout your Web site.

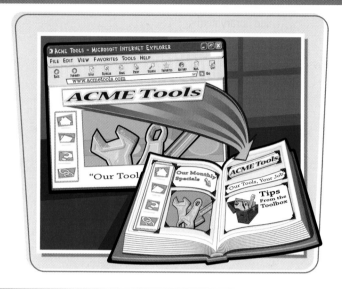

Create a Library Item

① Click and drag to select an element or collection of elements that you want to define as a library item.

Note: *Before you can use the library item feature in Dreamweaver, you must first set up and define your local site. To set up a local site, see Chapter 2.*

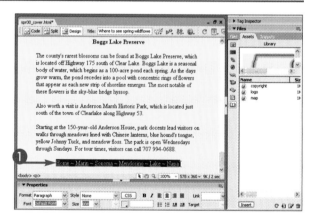

② Click **Modify**.

③ Click **Library**.

④ Click **Add Object to Library**.

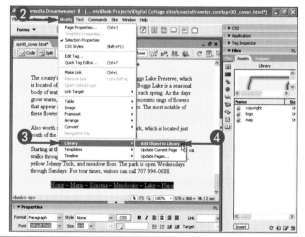

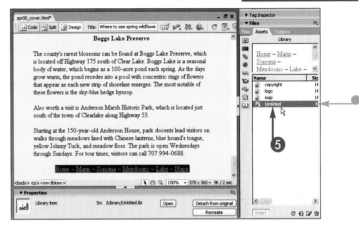

● A new untitled library item appears in the Library window.

⑤ Type a name for the library item.

⑥ Press Enter (Return).

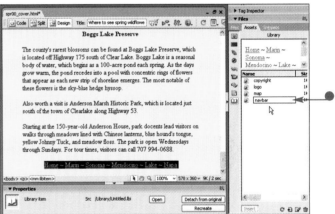

● The named library item appears in the Assets panel.

Defining an element as a library item prevents you from editing it in the Document window.

TIPS

What page elements should I make into library items?

Anything that appears multiple times in a Web site is a good candidate to become a library item. These elements include headers, footers, navigational menus, contact information, and disclaimers. Any element that appears in the body of an HTML document, including text, images, tables, forms, layers, and multimedia, may be defined as a library item.

Can I use multiple library items on the same HTML page?

There is no limit to the number of library items that you can use on a page. If your Web site is very standardized, then there may be little on your page that is not a library item. For example, you can create a photo gallery where each page has the same layout, except for the photo.

Insert a Library Item

You can insert an element onto your page from the library to avoid having to create it from scratch. This also ensures that the element is identical to other instances of that library item in your Web site.

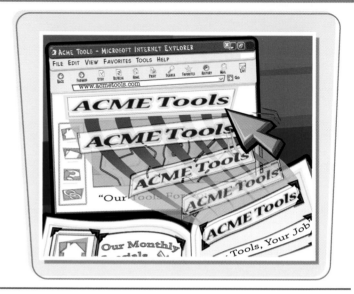

Insert a Library Item

① Position your mouse ⌖ where you want to insert the library item.

② Click **Window**.

③ Click **Assets**.

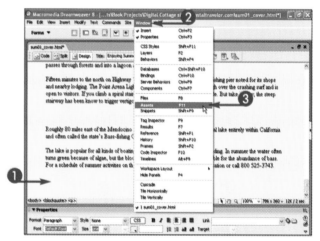

● The Assets panel opens.

● If the Library is not open in the Assets panel, you can click 🖽 to view the library.

④ Click a library item.

● The library item appears in the top of the Library window.

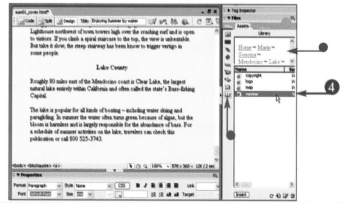

5 Click the menu in the Assets panel.

6 Click **Insert**.

You can also click and drag library items from the Library panel to the page to insert them.

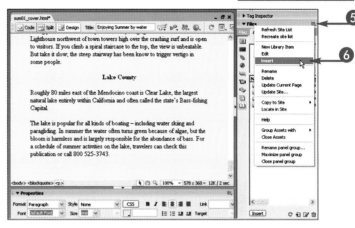

● Dreamweaver inserts the library item, in the Document window.

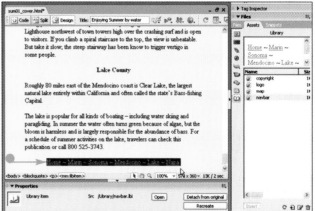

TIPS

How do I edit a library item that has been inserted into a page?

Instances of library items in your pages are locked and cannot be edited within the page. To edit a library item, you must either edit the original version of that item from the library, or detach the library item from the library to edit it within the page. However, if you detach the library item from the library, then the item is no longer a part of the library, and it is not updated when you change the library item.

Can I make an element a library item after I have used it on a few pages?

Yes. You can save any item to the library at any time. If you want to make sure that all instances of the item are attached to the library item, simply open any pages where you have already applied the item, delete it, and then insert it from the library.

Edit and Update a Library Item to Your Web Site

You can edit a library item and then automatically update all of the pages in your Web site that feature that item. This feature can help you save time when updating or redesigning a Web site.

Edit and Update a Library Item to Your Web Site

Note: *If the Assets panel is not open, see the section "View Library Items and Templates."*

① Double-click a library item to open it.

● The library item opens in a new window.

② Edit any element in the library item.

You can add or delete text, or insert tables.

In this example, the word County is being added to the end of each of the county names in the navigation bar.

③ Click **File**.

④ Click **Save**.

The Update Library Items dialog box appears, asking if you want to update all the instances of the library item in the site.

⑤ Click **Update**.

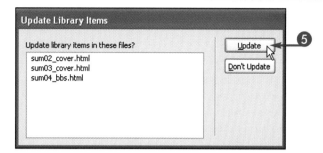

The Update Pages dialog box appears, showing the progress of the updates.

⑥ After Dreamweaver updates the site, click **Close**.

All instances of the applied library item are updated to reflect the changes made to the stored library item.

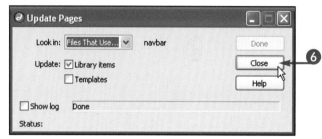

 TIPS

What do my pages look like after I have edited a library item and updated my Web site?

When you edit a library item and choose to update any instances of the library item that are already inserted into your Web pages, all of those instances are replaced with the edited versions. By using the library feature, you can make a change to a single library item and have multiple Web pages updated automatically.

Can I undo an update to a library item?

Technically, no. When you update pages with the library feature, the undo command does not undo all of the instances of these changes. However, you can go back to the Assets panel, open the library item, change it back to the way it was, and then apply those changes to all of the pages again.

Detach Library Content for Editing

You can detach an inserted library item from the original stored library item and then edit it as you would edit any other element in a Web page. If you detach a library item, then you can no longer make automatic updates when you change the original stored library item.

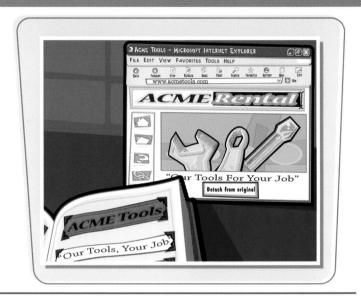

Detach Library Content for Editing

① Click to select the library item that you want to edit independently.

② Click **Detach from original**.

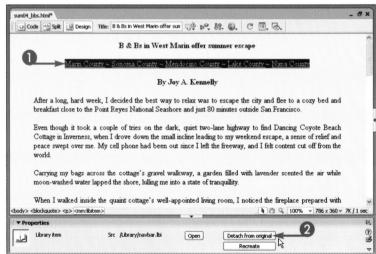

A warning dialog box appears.

③ Click **OK**.

● You can stop the warning from appearing each time that you perform this action by clicking the **Don't warn me again** check box (☐ changes to ☑).

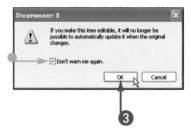

The element is no longer a library item and has no distinctive highlighting.

④ Click where you want to edit the library item, and make any edits that you want.

● You can add, delete, and format text. In this example, the font is changed.

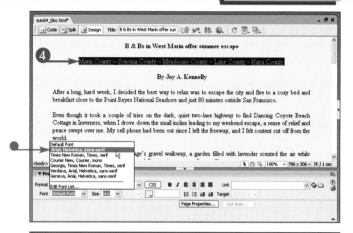

● Dreamweaver applies the editing to the text, image, or other element within the page.

Note: *Editing a detached library item has no effect on library items that are used on other pages.*

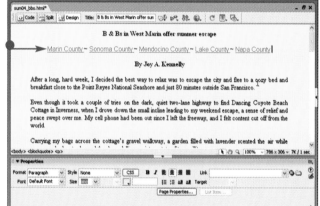

TIPS

When would I use the Detach from original command?

This command is useful when you use library items as partial page templates for specific design elements. For example, if you plan to have many captioned images in your Web site, you can create a library item with a two-celled table that contains a generic image and a formatted text caption. As a result, rather than recreating the table every time you want to add an image, you can insert the library item and then detach it from the library to make it editable. You can then replace the generic image and caption with appropriate content, as the formatting and design are done for you.

Can you reattach a library item?

Not exactly, but you can always reinsert a library item into a page and then delete the unattached library item. As a result, any changes that you make to the stored version are applied to the newly inserted version. Inserting a library item again may be faster than making the updates manually.

Create a Template

Templates are one of the most powerful and timesaving features in Dreamweaver because they enable you to create page designs that can be reused over and over again. Templates can also help you create more consistent designs for your pages.

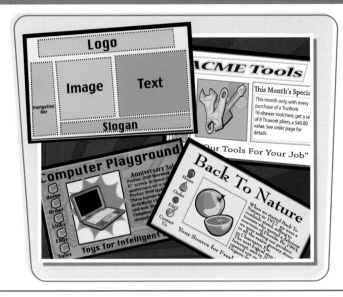

Create a Template

Note: *To create templates for your Web pages, you must already have defined a local Web site. To set up a local Web site, see Chapter 2.*

① Create and design a new page, or open the page that serves as a template.

● You can add placeholders where information changes from page to page.

② Click **File**.

③ Click **Save as Template**.

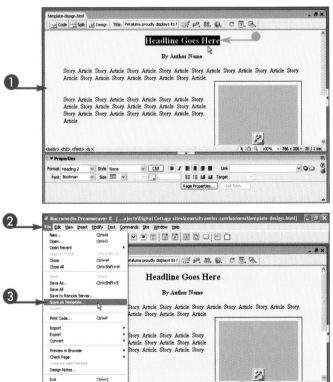

The Save As Template dialog box appears.

④ Click here and select your site name.

⑤ Type a name for the template.

⑥ Click **Save**.

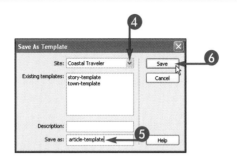

● The new template appears in the Templates window of the Assets panel.

If a template folder does not already exist, Dreamweaver automatically creates one to which it saves the new template.

Note: To make the template functional, you must define the editable regions where you want to modify content. For more information, see the section "Set an Editable Region in a Template."

TIPS

Can I create as many pages as I want from a template?

Yes. There is no limit to the number of pages that you can create from one template. In fact, the more pages that you plan to create using the same design, the more reason you have to save that design as a template, so that it does not have to be recreated each time.

How do you edit a page that is created with a template?

After you create a new Web page based on a template, you can only change the parts of the new page that are defined as editable. To change locked content, you must edit the original template. For more information about creating editable regions in a template, see the section "Set an Editable Region in a Template."

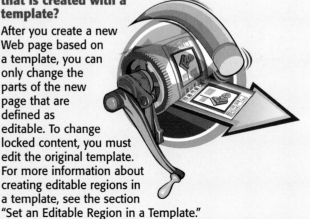

Set an Editable Region in a Template

After you create a Web page template, you must define which regions of the template are editable. When you create a page from the template, you can then edit these regions. Any areas of the template that are not set as editable cannot be changed in any pages that you create from the template.

Set an Editable Region in a Template

① Click **Window**.

② Click **Assets**.

The Files panel appears with the Assets tab visible.

③ Click 📖.

④ Double-click a template name to open it.

The template opens in the work area.

⑤ Click and drag to select the element that you want to define as editable.

⑥ Click **Insert**.

⑦ Click **Template Objects**.

⑧ Click **Editable Region**.

The New Editable Region dialog box appears.

9 Type a name for the editable region that distinguishes it from other editable regions on the page.

Note: You cannot use the characters &, ", ', <, or > in the name.

10 Click **OK**.

● A light blue box indicates the editable region, and a tab shows the region name.

11 Repeat Steps **5** to **10** for all of the regions on the page that you want to be editable.

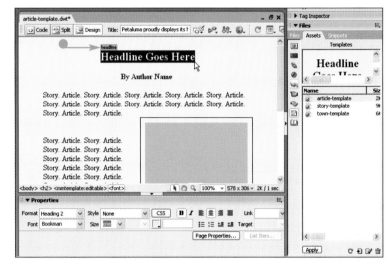

 TIPS

What parts of a template should be defined as editable?

You should define as editable any part of your template that you want to change from page to page. This can include headlines, stories, images, and captions that change from page to page. In contrast, you should lock site navigation, disclaimers, and copyright information that should be the same on all pages.

Can I use library items in my template pages?

Yes, you can use library items in templates. This is useful when you want to insert an item on pages that are made from the template. When you edit them, the library items update in the actual templates, and then in all of the pages that are created from those templates.

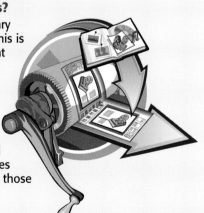

You can create a new Web page based on a template that you have already defined. This step saves you from having to build all of the generic elements that appear on many of your pages from scratch.

Create a Page From a Template

① Click **File**.

② Click **New**.

The New from Template dialog box appears.

③ Click the **Templates** tab.

④ Click to select the name of the Web site.

⑤ Click a template.

● A preview of the template appears in the dialog window.

⑥ Click **Create**.

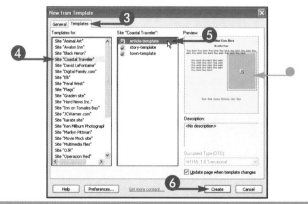

A new page is created from the template.

● The editable regions are surrounded by blue boxes.

⑦ Click in the editable areas and make any edits and changes to the page.

⑧ Type content into the editable regions.

⑨ Insert images into the editable regions.

⑩ Click **File**.

⑪ Click **Save** to save the template.

Dreamweaver saves the new page, based on the template.

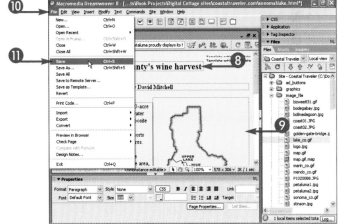

How do I detach a page from a template?

① Click **Modify**.

② Click **Templates**.

③ Click **Detach from Template**.

The page becomes a regular document with previously locked regions now fully editable. Edits to the original template no longer update the page.

Edit a Template and Update Your Web Site

When you make updates to a template file, Dreamweaver allows you the option to automatically update all of the pages that are created by the template. This enables you to make global changes to your Web site design in seconds.

Edit a Template and Update Your Web Site

① Click **Window**.

② Click **Assets**.

The Files panel appears with the Assets tab visible.

③ Click 🖼.

The available templates appear.

④ Double-click a template to open it.

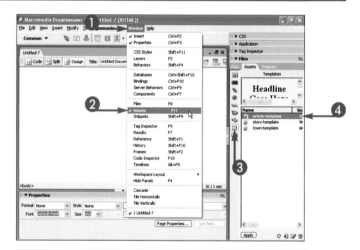

⑤ Click in the editable areas and make any edits that you want to the template.

● In this example, an editable region is added, formatted, and labeled with subheads.

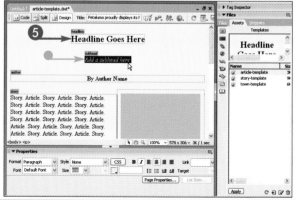

6 Click **File**.

7 Click **Save**.

The Update Template Files dialog box appears.

8 Click **Update**.

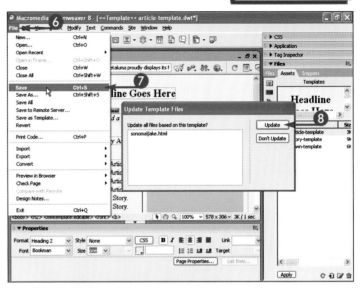

The Update Pages dialog box appears.

9 Click the Show log check box (☐ changes to ☑).

● The results of the update process appear in the Status pane.

10 After Dreamweaver updates the Web site, click **Close**.

All of the pages that use the template are updated to reflect the changes.

 TIPS

How does Dreamweaver store page templates?

Dreamweaver stores page templates in a folder called *Templates* inside the local site folder. You can open templates by clicking **File** and then clicking **Open**. In the Open dialog box, click ☑ and click the **Template** folder. You can click a template file to select it. You can also open templates from inside the Assets panel.

What are editable attributes?

Editable attributes allow you to change the properties of an element on a page. For example, you can give an image editable attributes, such as its source ALT text or size. Users need to keep the image on the page, and have the option to change things about the image. To use this feature, select an element, click **Modify**, then click **Templates**, and then click **Make Attribute Editable**.

12

Creating and Applying Cascading Style Sheets

This chapter shows you how to use Cascading Style Sheets to create and apply formatting. Cascading Style Sheets can save you a lot of tedious formatting time, especially on big Web sites.

Introduction to Cascading Style Sheets

You can apply many different types of formatting to your Web pages with style sheets, also known as *Cascading Style Sheets*, or *CSS*.

Format Text

CSS enables you to create as many different style sheets as you want. You can then use them to format text by applying multiple formatting options at once, such as font face, size, and color.

Create Global Web Page Styles

You can create style sheets that apply to all of the pages in your Web site. You can then use the same style across your pages to make the formatting more consistent. You can even make global changes by editing a style sheet to change the style across all of the pages that use the style.

HTML and Cascading Style Sheets

You can create custom Cascading Style Sheets, or you can redefine existing HTML tags to create custom styles. New styles can be applied to one page, or saved as external style sheets that you can apply across an entire Web site.

Embedded Style Sheets

A style sheet saved inside a particular Web page is an *embedded* style sheet. Embedded style sheet rules apply only to the page in which they are embedded.

External Style Sheets

When you want your style sheet to apply to all of the pages on your Web site, you must save it as a separate file called an *external* style sheet. You can use external style sheets to control formatting across multiple pages and even an entire Web site.

Style Sheets and Web Browsers

Some older Web browsers do not support style sheet standards, and different Web browsers display style sheets differently. Always test pages that use style sheets on different browsers to ensure that content displays as you intend it to for all of your visitors.

Customize an HTML Tag

You can customize the style that an existing HTML tag applies. This allows you to apply special formatting any time that you use that tag to format text. This is a quick, easy way to apply multiple style options with one HTML tag.

Not Customized ‹h1›   Customized ‹h1›

① Click **Text**.

② Click **CSS Styles**.

③ Click **New**.

The New CSS Rule dialog box appears.

④ Click the **Tag (redefines the look of a specific tag)** option (○ changes to ◉).

⑤ Click here and select a tag.

⑥ Click the **This document only** option to create an embedded style sheet for the file on which you are working (○ changes to ◉).

Note: To create style sheets for more than one document, see the section "Create an External Style Sheet."

⑦ Click **OK**.

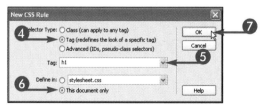

The CSS Rule definition dialog box appears.

⑧ Click a style category.

⑨ Select the style settings that you want.

⑩ Click **OK**.

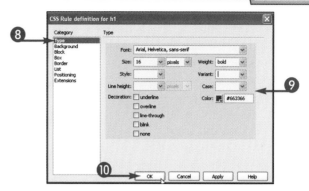

● Dreamweaver adds the new style to any content formatted with the redefined tag.

In this example, Heading 1 is redefined to use a different font face, color, and size.

● You can also apply the style by selecting content on the page and selecting the Heading 1 format.

Why should I redefine an HTML tag?

When you redefine an HTML tag, you can apply more than one style to the tag. As a result, you only have to use one HTML tag instead of several to apply multiple formatting options. For example, you can add center alignment to all your H1 tags to control the alignment of heading styles in one step. A special advantage to redefining HTML tags is that if a user's Web browser does not support style sheets, then the HTML tag still provides its basic formatting.

Does redefining an HTML tag change the format of any content that uses that tag?

Yes. When you redefine an HTML tag, you change the tag's formatting effect anywhere that you use the tag. You can limit the change to the page that you are working on, or you can include it in an external style sheet and apply it to an entire site. If you do not want to alter the style of an existing HTML tag, then you should create Class style sheets instead of redefining HTML tags. For more on Class style sheets, see the section "Create a Custom Style."

Create a Custom Style

You can create custom styles without affecting HTML tags. You can then apply those styles to text or other elements on your Web page, just as you would apply an HTML tag.

① Click **Text**.

② Click **CSS Styles**.

③ Click **New**.

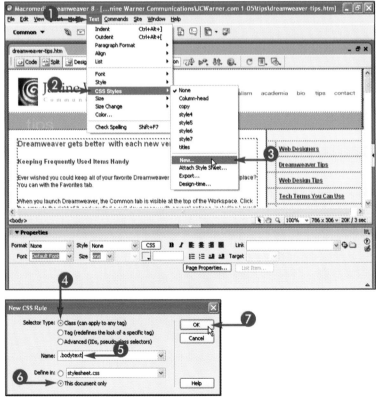

The New CSS Rule dialog box appears.

④ Click the **Class (can apply to any tag)** option (○ changes to ◉).

⑤ Type a name for the style.

Note: *Custom style names must begin with a period (.).*

⑥ Click the **This document only** option (○ changes to ◉).

Note: *To create style sheets for more than one document, see the section "Create an External Style Sheet."*

⑦ Click **OK**.

The CSS Rule definition dialog box appears.

⑧ Click a style category.

⑨ Select the style settings that you want.

⑩ Click **OK**.

The CSS Rule definition dialog box closes.

⑪ Click **Window**.

⑫ Click **CSS Styles**.

The CSS Styles panel opens, displaying the new style.

In this example, a font style setting is created. You can apply the new style to new or existing content.

Note: To apply a style sheet, see the section "Apply a Style."

TIPS

How does customizing an HTML tag differ from creating a custom style?

Customizing an HTML tag links a style to an existing HTML tag. The new style affects every instance of that tag. For example, if you customize your paragraph tags as green, then every paragraph in your page is green. With custom styles, you can apply styles that are independent of HTML tags and use them only where you want them.

Is it better to customize an HTML tag or create my own custom styles?

The advantage to redefining HTML tags is that you or your page designers do not have to keep track of new styles. On the other hand, there may be times when you need to use the HTML tag without the style. In these situations, custom styles may be a better solution.

Apply a Style

You can apply a style sheet to elements on your Web page to change their color, font, size, background, and other characteristics. This technique enables you to format elements without using standard HTML.

APPLY A STYLE TO AN ELEMENT

Note: To create a new custom style, see the section "Create a Custom Style."

① Click and drag to select text or another element to which you want to apply a style.

② In the Properties inspector, click the **Style** ☑.

③ Click the name of a style.

● Dreamweaver applies the style.

In this example, a font style is applied.

APPLY A STYLE TO THE ENTIRE BODY OF A PAGE

① Click inside the Document window.

② Click **<body>** in the tag Launcher area.

③ In the Properties inspector, click the **Style** 📋.

④ Click the name of the style.

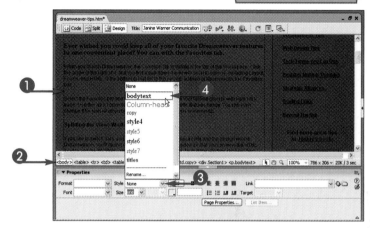

● Dreamweaver applies the new style sheet to the entire body of the page in the Document window.

In this example, a font style is applied to change the font face of all of the text on the page.

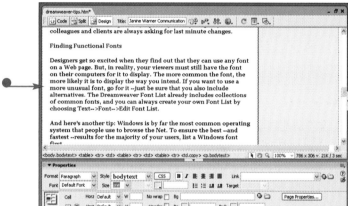

TIPS

What are some other options that I can use to define the formatting for text with a style sheet?

With style sheets, you can specify a numeric value for font weight. This enables you to apply varying degrees of boldness, instead of just a single boldness setting as with HTML. You can also define type size in absolute units, such as pixels, points, picas, inches, centimeters, or millimeters, or in relative units, such as ems, exs, or percentage.

Can I create as many style sheets as I want?

Yes. You can create as many style sheets as you want. However, one of the goals of style sheets is to help you work more efficiently, and so you should generally use them for formatting options that you want to apply many times within a document or Web site.

Edit a Style

You can edit style sheet definitions. You can then automatically apply the changes across all of the text or other elements to which you have applied the style on your page or Web site.

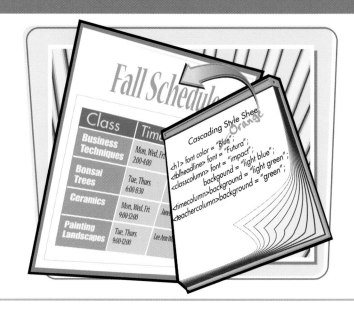

Edit a Style

① Click **Window**.

② Click **CSS Styles**.

● The CSS Styles panel opens, displaying all of the available styles.

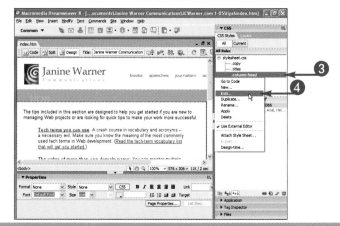

③ Right-click the name of a style that you want to edit.

④ Click **Edit**.

The CSS Rule Definition dialog box opens.

5 Click a style category.

6 Select the style settings that you want.

In this example, the font color is changed.

7 Click **OK**.

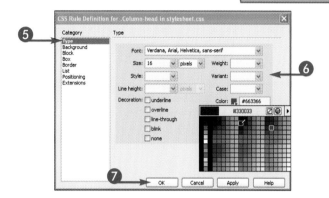

Dreamweaver saves the style sheet changes and automatically applies them anywhere that you have used the style.

● In this example, the font color changes when the new style definition is applied.

TIP

How can I implement CSS styles in HTML code?

You can implement CSS styles in one of three ways: by adding the <CLASS> attribute, the <SPAN> tag, or the <DIV> tag. First, you can simply add the <CLASS> attribute to any existing HTML tag. Whatever is affected by that tag uses the style that is specified by the class. The <SPAN> tag allows you to implement a style independently of any HTML on the page and without affecting the page layout. The <DIV> tag actually defines blocks of content, which then take on the style attributes defined in the <DIV> tag. <DIV> tags are very powerful and can actually be used for absolute positioning, similar to layers; they can even replace HTML tables. For more on layers, see Chapter 13.

Create Custom Link Styles

You can use style sheet *selectors* to customize the links on your page. Selectors enable you to customize your links in ways that you cannot with HTML. For example, they can remove the underline from linked text, which many designers find distracting.

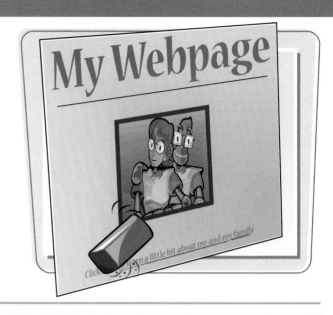

Create Custom Link Styles

① Click **Text**.

② Click **CSS Styles**.

③ Click **New**.

The New CSS Rule dialog box appears.

④ Click the **Advanced (IDs, pseudo-class selectors)** option (○ changes to ◉).

⑤ Click here and select a selector.

⑥ Click the **This document only** option to create an embedded style sheet (○ changes to ◉).

Note: To create style sheets for more than one document, see the section "Create an External Style Sheet."

⑦ Click **OK**.

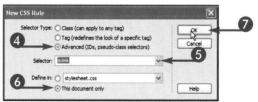

The CSS Rule definition dialog box appears.

⑧ Click the **Type** style category.

⑨ Click here to select the style settings that you want.

● To remove underlining from links, you can click **none** under the Decoration section (☐ changes to ☑).

⑩ Click **OK**.

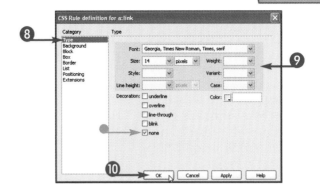

Dreamweaver applies the style changes to all links on the page.

● In this example, the column headlines are no longer underlined, even though they are all links.

What are some non-text based features that I can implement with style sheets?

Probably the most exciting thing that you can do with style sheets is to position elements precisely on the page. Style sheets allow you freedom from traditional, and imprecise, layout methods, such as HTML tables. Style sheets use the <DIV> tag, which defines an area on the page where you can position an element with alignment attributes, and more precisely by specifying an actual pixel location in the page.

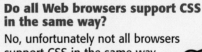

Do all Web browsers support CSS in the same way?

No, unfortunately not all browsers support CSS in the same way, and some do not support styles at all. However, styles have come a long way in the last few years and so have browsers. Although some visitors may not be able to see your designs as you intend if you use CSS, the vast majority of people surfing the Web these days have browsers that support CSS.

Create an External Style Sheet

External style sheets enable you to define a set of style sheet rules and then apply them to many different pages — even pages on different Web sites. This allows you to keep a consistent appearance across many pages, and streamline formatting and style updates.

Create an External Style Sheet

① Click **Text**.

② Click **CSS Styles**.

③ Click **New**.

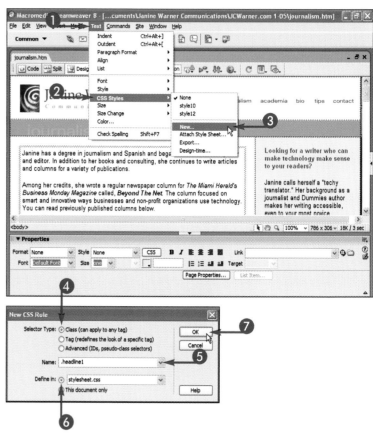

The New CSS Rule dialog box appears.

④ Click the **Class (can apply to any tag)** option (○ changes to ◉).

⑤ Type a name for the style.

Note: *Class names must begin with a period (.).*

⑥ Click the **Define in** option (○ changes to ◉).

⑦ Click **OK**.

The CSS Rule Definition dialog box appears.

⑧ Click a category.

⑨ Click here and select the style settings that you want.

⑩ Click **OK**.

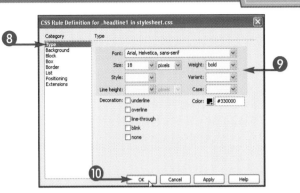

Dreamweaver saves the style to the external style sheet and automatically creates a folder named CSS in your site folder.

If this is the first external style sheet that you are defining, then Dreamweaver prompts you to save the CSS file and creates it automatically.

Note: The external style sheet is created inside your local site folder. For this to work, you must have defined your site in Dreamweaver.

For more information on defining a site and identifying the local site folder, see Chapter 2.

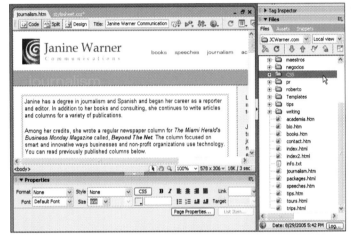

TIP

How can I export an internal style sheet?

① Click **Text**.

② Click **CSS Styles**.

③ Click **Export**.

The Export Styles As CSS File dialog box appears.

④ Click ⌄ and select a location to save the CSS file.

⑤ Type a name for the file.

⑥ Click **Save**.

Dreamweaver exports the internal styles to the new external style sheet, which you can then apply to other pages.

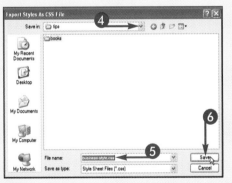

Note: To apply the style sheet to a new page, see the section Apply a Style.

Attach an External Style Sheet

Any style sheet that you create becomes accessible from the Properties inspector Style field. Creating style sheets for common formatting options makes it easy to apply complicated styles with a single click. You must attach the style sheet first before you can apply the styles to the content on your page.

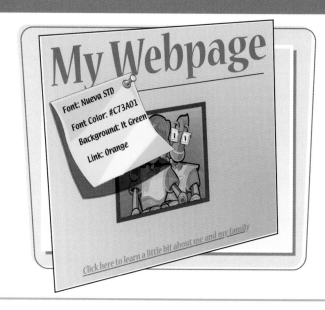

Attach an External Style Sheet

① In the page to which you want to attach a style sheet, click **Text**.

② Click **CSS Styles**.

③ Click **Attach Style Sheet**.

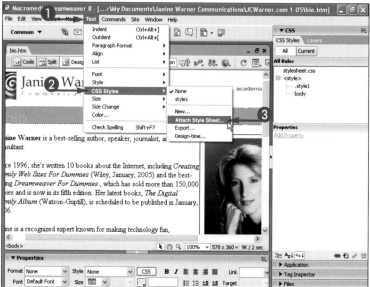

● The Attach External Style Sheet dialog box appears with the name of your open file to which you want to attach the style sheet.

④ Click **OK**.

The External Style Sheet is associated with the page, and you can apply any styles from the style sheet to the page.

The styles from the Sheet File become available from the Properties inspector.

5 Select any text or other element to which you want to apply a style.

6 In the Properties inspector, click the **Style** ⌄.

7 Click the name of a style that you want to apply.

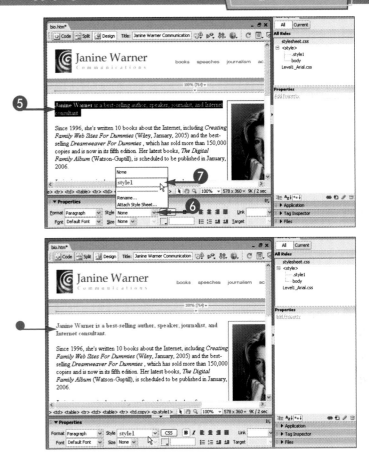

● Dreamweaver applies the style.

Note: To apply styles to content in a document, see the section "Apply a Style."

How can I add more styles to an external style sheet?

For the steps on how to add more styles to an existing external style sheet, see the section "Create a Custom Style." To customize an HTML tag, see the section "Customize an HTML Style." You must also ensure that you define the style as an external style sheet. When you define a new style as an external style, it is automatically added to the external style sheet.

Is it possible to add new styles later?

Yes. You can add styles to an external style sheet at any point during production, even months after the site was first published. In addition, you can make changes or additions while you work on any page that is currently attached to the external style sheet.

You can include hundreds of styles in a single external sheet. This allows you to continue to add to the style sheet as your site grows, and to change or add sections.

Edit an External Style Sheet

Note: *If the Styles panel is not open, from the menu click Window and then click Styles to open it.*

① Click to select a style in the CSS Styles panel.

● The style properties appear.

② Right-click and select the name of a style.

You can also edit the style by clicking any of the properties, and entering a different value.

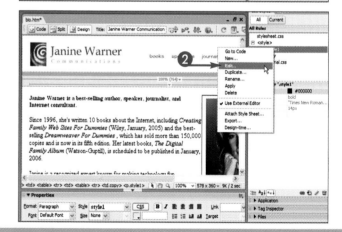

The CSS Rule definition dialog box appears.

③ Click a style category.

④ Click here and select the style settings that you want.

In this example, the font size is changed.

⑤ Click **OK**.

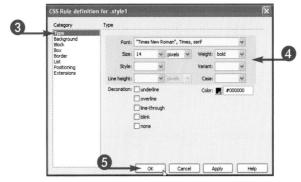

Dreamweaver saves the style to the external style sheet.

⑥ Click to select text or another element.

⑦ In the Properties inspector, click the **Style** ☑.

⑧ Click the name of a style.

Dreamweaver applies the style to the element.

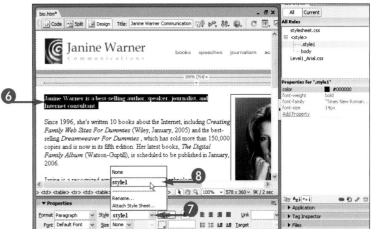

What problems can arise when I use CSS?

The benefits to using Cascading Style Sheets are enormous, and they mostly outweigh the small problems that come with their implementation. However, this does not mean that you can ignore those problems completely. First, watch out for browser support. Some CSS specifications simply are not completely reliable across browsers, and so you should always test your pages to make sure that you like the results. Second, the user pays the price for the increased design control. For example, if you are using text CSS controls to set your font size in pixels and points, users will no longer be able to increase the text size when they browse. This may mean decreased usability, depending on your audience.

Using Layers to Increase User Interaction

In addition to other layout tools, Dreamweaver allows you to quickly create layers. This chapter shows you how to gain more design control and increase user interaction using the Layers feature.

You can use advanced Dreamweaver tools to create layers and then stack them on top of each other for more precise layout control. You can also add scripting with Dreamweaver behaviors to increase the interactivity of your Web site.

Layer Basics

Layers are discrete blocks of content that you can precisely position on the page, make moveable by the user, and even make invisible. Most significantly, you can stack layers on top of each other. Layers can contain any kind of content, including text, graphics, tables — even other layers. Unfortunately, because layers are so new to HTML, they are not supported in the same way by all Web browsers, and so you may need to do more testing to ensure that your pages work properly.

Nested Layers

Layers can contain nested layers, which create areas of content that stay linked together on a page for better control during production of Web pages. Nested, or child, layers can inherit the properties of their parent layers, including visibility or invisibility. You can also nest layers within other nested layers. Keep in mind that using nested layers is one of the most problematic design options because not all Web browsers support nested layers.

Behavior Basics

Behaviors are cause-and-effect events that you can insert into your Web pages. For example, creative behaviors can make pictures on a Web page change, or a new Web browser window open when a user clicks or positions a mouse over an object. Logical behaviors tell people which Web browser they are using, or remind them to fill out their name in your Web site questionnaire form.

Behind the Scenes

Dreamweaver behaviors insert brief programs called *scripts* into your Web pages. Dreamweaver creates these scripts in a language called *JavaScript*; however, many available behaviors rely on other technologies such as ActiveX and SSI. JavaScript is by far the most accepted and widely used browser-side programming language due to its wide browser acceptance and powerful capabilities.

Behaviors and Browsers

Because behaviors vary in complexity, they are written in various ways to ensure compatibility with older Web browsers. Both Internet Explorer and Netscape Navigator adopted the majority of DHTML and JavaScript technologies after version 4 of each of these browsers. However, each Web browser's behavior may still vary. Dreamweaver enables you to disable behaviors that may not work in older Web browsers.

Check Browser Versions

In order to design a page that works equally well in all Web browsers, you have to refrain from using the latest available Web-design technologies. Some of the features in this chapter are not available for older Web browser versions. You can create two versions of your site — one for new browsers and one for older browsers — and Dreamweaver can automatically redirect users to the page that is appropriate for their browser. However, you will have a lot more work maintaining two versions of your site than one version.

Create a Layer with Content

Layers are scalable rectangles, inside of which you can place text and pictures. Although they work similar to tables by providing design control, they are much more precise. If you have worked with the Layer feature in Adobe Photoshop, then you may find that HTML layers are similar.

Unlike other elements in HTML, layers can be placed anywhere on a page, and they can also overlap other layers.

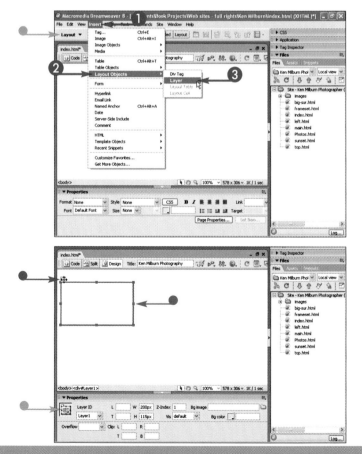

Create a Layer with Content

CREATE A LAYER

① Click **Insert**.

② Click **Layout Objects**.

③ Click **Layer**.

● You can also insert layers from the Layout Insert bar.

● The outline of the layer appears.

● You can click the tab in the upper-left corner of the layer to select it.

● When you select the layer, the Properties inspector displays the layer's properties.

ADD CONTENT TO A LAYER

1. Click inside the layer (⬚ changes to I).

2. Type text into the layer.

● You can format text within a layer using the Properties inspector, just as you would format text on a page.

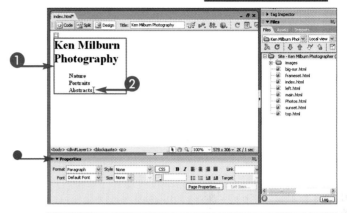

3. Add an image by clicking **Insert Image** (🖳).

● In this example, the text and image are inside the same layer.

You can specify image properties, such as alignment within a layer.

Note: To format text, see Chapter 5. For image options, see Chapter 7. To insert and format tables, see Chapter 9.

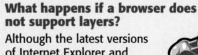

TIPS

Should I use layers instead of HTML tables?

Layers are very powerful layout tools that offer a page designer better control over the placement of content on a Web page. However, layers are not fully supported by all Web browsers, and so, many Web designers continue to use tables to create page designs. It is important to know the type and version of browser that your visitors are using when you are deciding whether to use layers or tables.

What happens if a browser does not support layers?

Although the latest versions of Internet Explorer and Netscape support layers, older browsers that do not support layers simply ignore them. Unfortunately, this means that if someone views your page using an older browser, then any content, such as text or images, that you place inside a layer, is not visible.

Resize and Reposition Layers

When you create a new layer, you can adjust its position and dimensions to make it fit attractively within the rest of the content on your page. One of the advantages of layers is that you can move them easily, by clicking and dragging them.

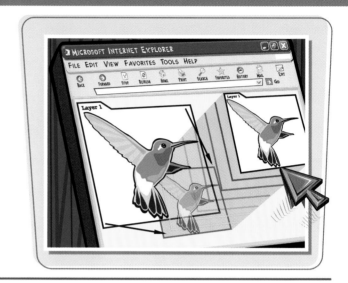

Resize and Reposition Layers

CLICK AND DRAG TO RESIZE A LAYER

① Click the tab in the upper-left corner of the layer to select it.

● Square, black handles appear around the edges of the layer.

② Click and drag one of the handles.

Dreamweaver resizes the layer to the new size.

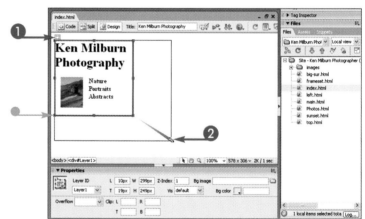

RESIZE WITH WIDTH AND HEIGHT ATTRIBUTES

① Click the tab in the upper-left corner of the layer to select it.

② Type a new measurement into the W (Width) field.

③ Press **Enter** (**Return**).

Dreamweaver changes the layer's width.

④ Type a new measurement into the H (Height) field.

⑤ Press **Enter** (**Return**).

Dreamweaver changes the layer's height.

● You can also type **in** for inches or **cm** for centimeters next to the height and width.

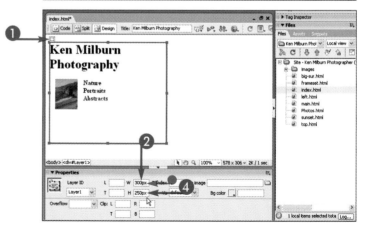

REPOSITION WITH THE CURSOR

1 Click and drag the tab in the upper-left corner of the layer to move it to a new position.

Dreamweaver moves the layer to the new location.

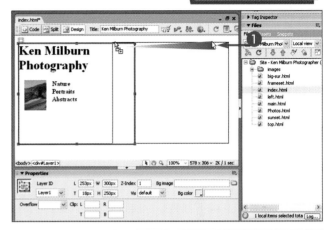

REPOSITION WITH LEFT AND TOP ATTRIBUTES

1 Click the tab in the upper-left corner of the layer to select it.

2 Type the new distance from the top of the window in the T (Top) field.

3 Type the new distance from the left side of the window in the L (Left) field.

Dreamweaver applies the new positioning to the layer.

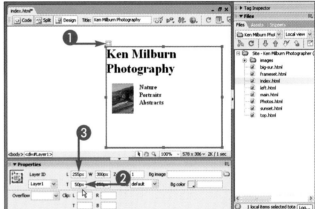

TIPS

How can I change the visibility of a layer?

To change a layer's visibility, select a layer and then click the **Vis** ⊡ in the Property inspector. You can make a layer visible or invisible, or if it is a nested layer, then it can inherit its characteristics from its parent, which is the enclosing layer.

Is there any other way to tell if a layer is visible or invisible?

There is a visibility column available in the Layers panel. Click next to the layer name in the visibility column to adjust it. The open eye (👁) means the layer is visible; the closed eye (👁) means the layer is invisible. If no icon is showing, visibility is set to the default, and the layer appears visible, or inherits its visibility.

Change the Stacking Order of Layers

You can change the stacking order of layers on a page, thus affecting how they overlap one another. You can then hide parts of some layers under other layers.

Change the Stacking Order of Layers

CHANGE ORDER IN THE LAYERS PANEL

If the Layers panel is not open, click **Window** and then click **Layers** to open it.

① Click and drag the layer name in the Layers panel above or below another layer (⤢ changes to ⤢).

Dreamweaver changes the stacking order of the layers.

● Notice the difference in Z-Index values in the Layers panel.

CHANGE THE ORDER WITH THE Z-INDEX ATTRIBUTE

① Click the tab in the upper-left corner of a layer to select it.

② Type a new number in the Z-Index field.

Layers with greater Z-Index values are placed higher in the stack.

Dreamweaver changes the stacking order of the layers.

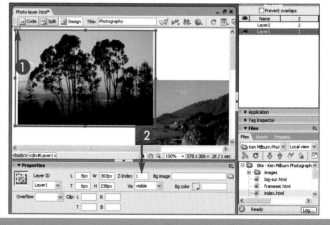

Using Dreamweaver behaviors and layers, you can enable visitors to interact with layers, play sound files, and add pop-up messages.

Add a Behavior to a Layer

If the Behaviors panel is not open, click **Window** and then click **Layers** to open it.

① Click ⊞ in the Behaviors panel.

② In the pop-up menu that appears, click **Play Sound**.

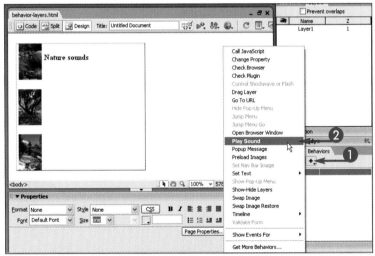

The Play Sound dialog box appears.

③ Click **Browse** and select a sound file.

④ Click **OK**.

The sound file is automatically associated with the layer and plays when the page is displayed in a Web browser.

Note: To preview a page in a Web browser, see Chapter 2.

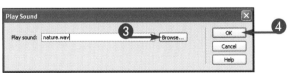

Create Complex Designs with Layers

You can create complex page designs using layers to position elements precisely. Using drag and drop, you can move layers to any place on a page.

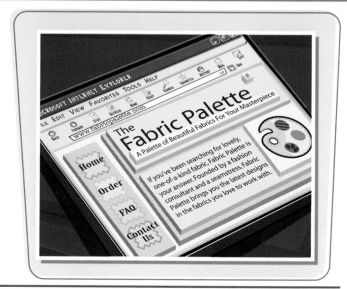

If the Layout bar is not open, click here and select **Layout**.

① Click **Layers** (▨) in the Layout bar.

② Click and drag to create a layer.

③ Add content to the layer.

④ Click ▨ in the Layout bar.

⑤ Click and drag to create a second layer.

⑥ Add content to the new layer.

You can repeat Steps **3** to **6** to create additional layers with content.

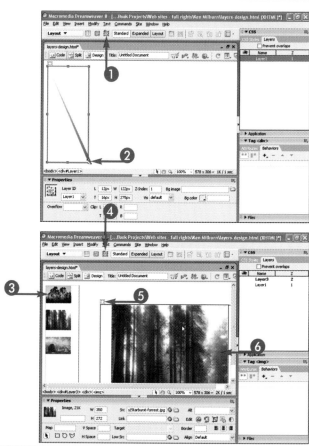

⑦ Click to select a layer.

⑧ Drag and drop layers until they are where you want them on the page.

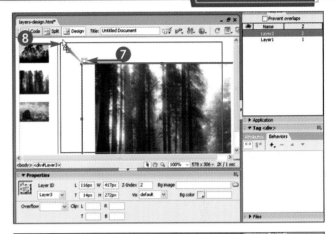

● The layers are positioned on the page.

Keep in mind that not all Web browsers support layers in the same way, and so you should test in multiple browsers.

Note: *To learn more about previewing a page in a Web browser, see Chapter 2.*

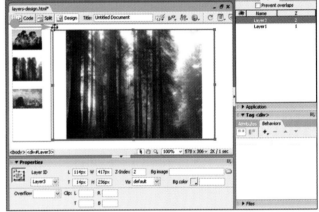

TIPS

Can I add as many layers as I want to a page?

Yes. You can add as many layers as you want to a page, and add as much content as you want to any given layer. You can also position the layers anywhere you want on a page, moving them around until you have the design you want.

Can I place a layer inside another layer?

Yes. You can create nested layers so that you can place a layer inside another layer to create an even more complex page design. See the section "Create a Nested Layer" for more information.

Create a Nested Layer

A nested layer is often called a child layer, and the layer that contains a nested layer is the parent layer. They act as a unit on the page; if the parent layer moves, the child goes with it. You can move the child layer independently of the parent, but the layers always stay linked.

① Click ▤ in the Layout bar.

② Click and drag to create a layer.

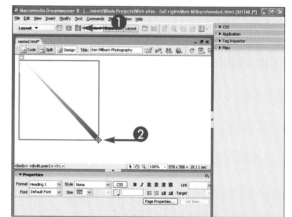

Dreamweaver inserts a layer into the page.

You can insert text, images, or tables into the layer. In this example, text is placed in the first layer.

③ Click inside the current layer.

④ Click **Insert**.

⑤ Click **Layout Objects**.

⑥ Click **Layer**.

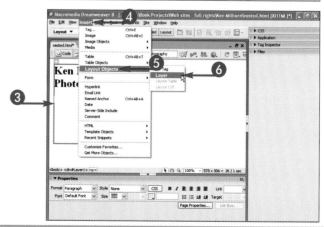

● Dreamweaver inserts a nested layer into the first layer.

You can insert text, images, or tables into the layer. In this example, an image and some text are placed in the nested layer.

⑦ Click and drag to position the layers on the page.

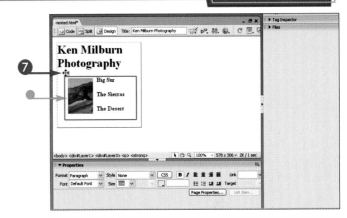

⑧ Click **Window**.

⑨ Click **Layers**.

The Layers panel opens.

● Both layers appear. The L symbol before the layer indicates that the second layer, labeled Layer3 in this example, is nested inside Layer1.

TIP

Can I free a nested layer?
Yes, you can take a nested layer out of its parent layer. Click **Window** and then click **Layers** to open the Layers panel. Click the nested layer and drag it above the parent layer. The layer is no longer nested.

Publishing a Web Site

You can publish your completed Web pages on a server to allow the world to view them. This chapter shows you how to publish your Web site, and keep it up-to-date with Dreamweaver.

Publish Your Web Site

To make the Web pages that you have built in Dreamweaver accessible on the Web, you must transfer them to a Web server. A *Web server* is an Internet-connected computer running special software that enables the computer to serve files to Web browsers. Dreamweaver includes tools that enable you to connect and transfer pages to a Web server.

Steps for Publishing Your Web Site

To publish your site content using Dreamweaver, follow these steps:

① Specify where on your computer the site files are kept.

Note: To define a local site, see Chapter 2.

② Specify the Web server to which you want to publish your files.

Note: To define a remote site, see the section "Set Up a Remote Site."

Most people publish their Web pages on servers maintained by their Internet service provider (ISP), a hosting company, or their company or school.

③ Connect to the Web server and transfer the files.

The Site window gives you a user-friendly interface for organizing your files and transferring them to the remote site.

After uploading your site, you can update it by editing the copies of the site files on your computer (the local site) and then transferring those copies to the Web server (the remote site).

With the Site window, you can view the organization of all files in your site. You can also upload local files to the remote site and download remote files to the local site through the Files panel. You can access the Site window by clicking the Expand/Collapse button in the Files panel. For more information about the Files panel, see Chapter 3.

Local Files

The right pane displays the content of your site, as it exists on your local computer. To define a local site, see Chapter 2.

Remote Site

The left pane displays the content of your site as it exists on the remote Web server. To define a remote site, see the section "Set Up a Remote Site."

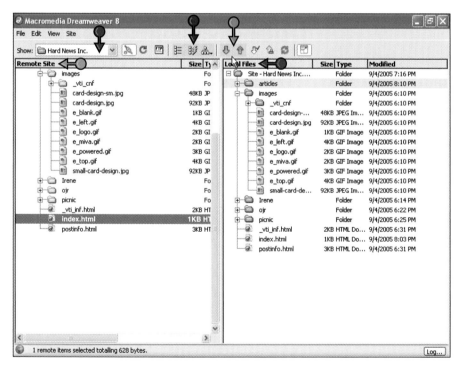

File Transfer

These buttons enable you to connect to your remote site, refresh the file list, upload files to the remote server, download files to the local site, and view the FTP log.

Site Menu

This menu allows you to select from the different sites that you have defined in Dreamweaver. For more about defining sites in Dreamweaver, see Chapter 2.

Site Window View

You can click 🔠 or 🔠 to switch between viewing your site as a list of files or as a site map. You can click 🔢 to access a Testing Server. For more about using the site map view, see Chapter 15.

Test Your Pages in Different Browsers

There are still big differences between how HTML pages display in different browsers and different browser versions. You can preview an HTML page in any browser that is installed on your computer.

① Click **File**.

② Click **Preview in Browser**.

③ Click **Edit Browser List**.

The Preferences dialog box appears.

④ Click ⊞ in the Preview in Browser area.

The Add Browser dialog box appears.

⑤ Click **Browse**.

The Select Browser dialog box appears.

6 Click here and select the folder that contains a browser application.

7 Click the browser application that you want to add.

8 Click **Open**.

The Select Browser dialog box closes.

9 Click **OK** to add the browser and close the Add Browser dialog box.

10 Repeat Steps **4** to **9** to add additional browsers.

11 Click **OK** to accept your preferences and close the Preferences dialog box.

You can click the **Preview in Browser** icon () in the Document toolbar to preview an HTML page in any browser that you have added.

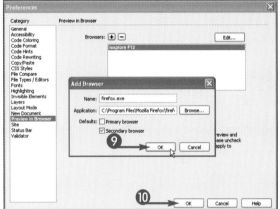

TIPS

Where can I download older versions of browsers that are still in use?

There are several browser archives on the Web, but one of the best is at http://browsers.evolt.org/, which has a comprehensive listing of current and discontinued browsers for all kinds of operating systems and versions.

What is the most popular browser?

There are dozens of browsers in use on the Web, including Netscape, Firefox, Opera, and even special browsers for the disabled that read Web pages to their users. However, the most popular browser these days, according to most sources, is Microsoft Internet Explorer.

Organize Your Files and Folders

You can use the Files panel to organize the files and folders that make up your Web site. With this panel, you can create and delete files and folders, as well as move files between folders; Dreamweaver automatically fixes any associated links.

Creating subfolders to organize files of a similar type can be useful if you have a large Web site.

Organize Your Files and Folders

MOVE SITE FILES

① Click **Window**.

② Click **Files**.

● The Files panel displays.

③ In the Files panel, click ▼ to display the contents of the site.

④ Click ⊞ to view the files in a subfolder (⊞ changes to ⊟).

● The folder contents display.

You can click ⊟ to close the subfolder.

⑤ Click and drag a file from the local site folder into a subfolder (⍐ changes to ⍌).

The Update Files dialog box appears, asking if you want to update your links.

⑥ Click **Update** to keep your local site links from breaking.

Dreamweaver automatically makes any changes necessary to preserve the links.

TIPS

What happens to links when I move files?

When you move files into and out of folders, you need to update any hyperlinks or images that are referenced on those pages, because these references can become broken. Dreamweaver keeps track of any affected code when you rearrange files in the Files panel, and it can update the code for you when you move a file. This feature can save you time and prevent your site links from breaking.

Should I use subfolders?

Organizing your text, image, and multimedia files in subfolders can help you keep track of the contents of your Web site. Although you can store all of the files on your site in one main directory, most designers find it easier to find files when the files are organized in subfolders.

Set Up a Remote Site

The *remote site* is what Dreamweaver calls your site on the Web server. Think of it as a place where your Web site is made available to the rest of the world. You can set up a remote site by specifying a directory on a Web server where your site will be hosted. You can then transfer your files from your computer to the remote server.

Set Up a Remote Site

① Click **Site**.

② Click **Manage Sites**.

The Manage Sites dialog box appears.

③ Click a site name from the list.

④ Click **Edit**.

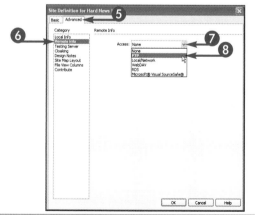

The Site Definition dialog box appears.

⑤ Click the **Advanced** tab.

⑥ Click **Remote Info**.

⑦ Click the **Access** ▾.

⑧ Click **FTP**.

FTP is the most common way for Web designers to connect to their Web servers. The other options are only used in special situations.

246

9 Type the name of the FTP host (Web server).

10 Type the directory path of your site on the Web server.

11 Type your login name and password.

You can click the **Enable file check in and check out** option if you want to work on the site collaboratively (□ changes to ✓), and enter a username and e-mail address.

12 Click **OK**.

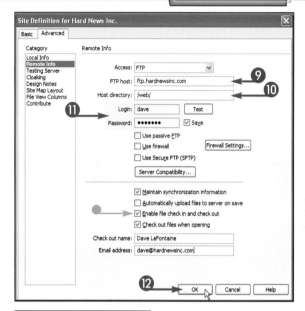

The Site Definition dialog box closes.

13 Click **Done**.

The remote site is now set up.

What happens if I change my Internet service provider (ISP) and I need to move my site to a different server?

You need to change your remote site settings to enable Dreamweaver to connect to your new ISP server. Your local site settings can stay the same. Make sure that you keep your local files current and backed up before you change servers.

How do I register a domain name?

You can register a domain name at a number of domain registration services on the Internet. Two of the most popular, and least expensive, are www.godaddy.com and www.1and1.com. As long as you pay the annual fee (less than $10 a year at these sites), the domain is yours. To direct the domain to your Web site, you need to specify where your Web server is at the domain registration service.

reservations:
WWW.GODADDY OR
WWW.1AND1.COM

Connect to a Remote Site

You can connect to the Web server that hosts your remote site and transfer files between it and Dreamweaver. Dreamweaver connects to the Web server by a process known as *File Transfer Protocol*, or *FTP*.

Before you can connect to a remote server, you need to set up your remote site. For more information, see the section "Set Up a Remote Site."

Connect to a Remote Site

① In the Files panel, click **Expand Site Panel** (🗗) to expand the remote and local site panels.

The Files panel expands to fill the screen.

② Click **Connect** (🖧) to connect to the Web server.

Note: Dreamweaver displays an alert dialog box if it cannot connect to the site. If you have trouble connecting, then double-check the host information that you entered for the remote site.

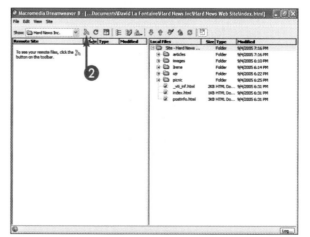

- The Connect button (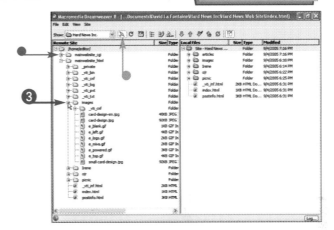) changes to the Disconnect button (), thereby, indicating a successful connection.

- Dreamweaver displays the contents of the remote site's host directory.

③ Click to view the content of a directory on the Web server (changes to).

Dreamweaver displays the contents of the directory.

④ Click **Disconnect** ().

Dreamweaver disconnects from the Web server.

If you do not transfer any files for 30 minutes, Dreamweaver automatically disconnects from a Web server.

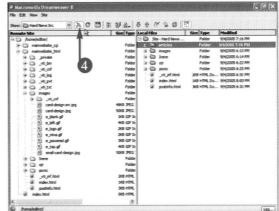

TIPS

How do I keep Dreamweaver from prematurely disconnecting from the Web server?

You can click **Edit**, then click **Preferences**, and then click **Site**. You can adjust the FTP transfer options to change the time that Dreamweaver allows to pass between commands before it logs you off the server — the default is 30 minutes. Note that Web servers also have a similar setting on their end. Therefore, the server, not Dreamweaver, may sometimes log you off if you are inactive for more than the server's allotted time.

What if the connection does not work?

If Dreamweaver fails to connect to your server, then your Internet connection may be down. Make sure your computer is connected to the Internet and try again. If you still cannot connect, then you may have incorrectly entered the FTP settings. Check with your service provider or system administrator if you are not sure about your Web server settings.

Upload Files to a Web Server

You can use Dreamweaver's FTP features to upload files from your local site to your remote server, to make your Web pages available to others on the Internet.

Upload Files to a Web Server

① Click 🖾 to connect to the Web server through the Site window (🖾 changes to 🖾).

② Click the file or folder that you want to upload.

③ Click **Put** (⬆).

Note: *You can also right-click the file and select* ***Put*** *from the menu that appears.*

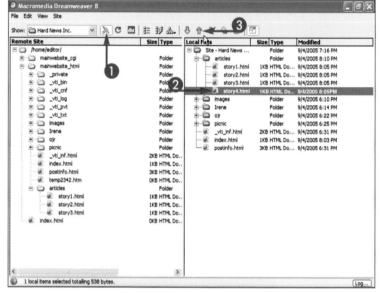

A dialog box appears, asking if you want to include dependent files.

Dependent files are images and other files associated with a particular page. If you are uploading a page that displays images, then those images are dependent files.

④ Click **Yes** or **No**.

● You can click the check box (☐ changes to ☑) to avoid seeing this dialog box in the future.

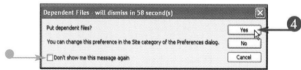

● The file transfers from your computer to the Web and the file name appears in the Remote files panel.

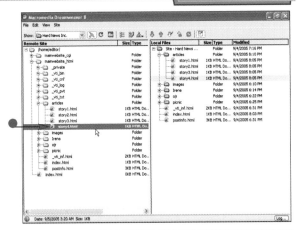

UPLOAD A FOLDER

1 In the right pane, right-click the folder (📁) that you want to upload.

2 Click **Put** in the menu that appears.

You can also click the 📁 and then click ⬆️.

Dreamweaver transfers the folder and its contents from your computer to the Web server.

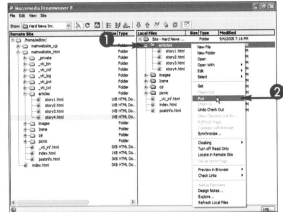

TIPS

How do I stop a file transfer in progress?

You can click **Cancel** from the Status window that appears while a transfer is in progress. You can also press Esc to cancel a file transfer.

How can I delete a file off the Web server?

With the Site window open, connect to the Web server. When the list of files appears in the left pane, click the file that you want to delete, and then press Delete. A dialog box appears, asking if you really want to delete the selected file. Click **OK**. You can also delete multiple files and folders.

Download Files from a Web Server

You can download files from your remote site in Dreamweaver if you need to retrieve them. Once they are downloaded, you can make changes or updates to the pages in Dreamweaver and then put them back on the Web server.

① Click 🖟 to connect to the Web server
(🖟 changes to 🖟).

② Click the file that you want to download.

③ Click **Get** (🖟).

Note: *You can also right-click the file in the remote site and select* **Get** *in the menu that appears.*

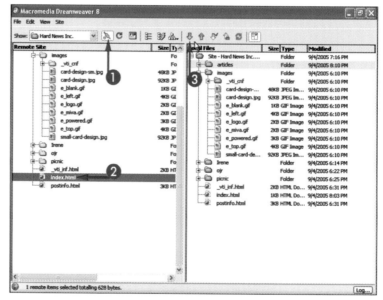

A dialog box appears, asking if you want to include dependent files.

Dependent files are images and other files associated with a particular page. If you are downloading a page that displays images, then those images are dependent files.

④ Click **Yes** or **No**.

● You can click the check box
(☐ changes to ☑) to avoid seeing this dialog box in the future.

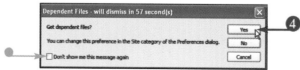

● The file transfers from the Web server to your computer.

If the file already exists on your local computer, then a dialog box appears, asking whether it is okay to overwrite it.

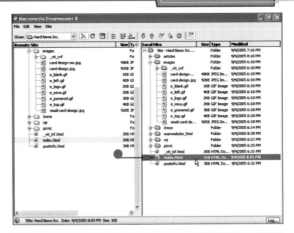

DOWNLOAD MULTIPLE FILES

① Press and hold Ctrl (Shift) and click to select the files that you want to download.

② Click 🔽.

The files transfer from your Web server to your computer.

TIPS

Where does Dreamweaver log errors that occur during transfer?

Dreamweaver logs all transfer activity, including errors, in a file-transfer log. You can view it by clicking **Window**, then clicking **Results**, and then clicking FTP **Log**. The FTP Log panel appears at the bottom of the screen.

Can I use my Web site to store files while I am still working on them?

If a file is on your Web server, then it can be viewed on the Internet. When pages are under construction and you do not want them to be seen, you should not put them up on your Web site, even temporarily. Even if the page is not linked to your site, someone may find it, or a search engine may even index and cache it.

Synchronize Your Local and Remote Sites

Dreamweaver can synchronize files between your local and remote sites so that both sites have an identical set of the most recent files. This can be useful if other people are editing the files on the remote site, and you need to update your local copies of those files. It is also handy if you edit pages and you do not remember all of the pages that you need to upload.

Synchronize Your Local and Remote Sites

① Click 🖳 to connect to the Web server
(🖳 changes to 🖳).

② Click **Synchronize** (🔃).

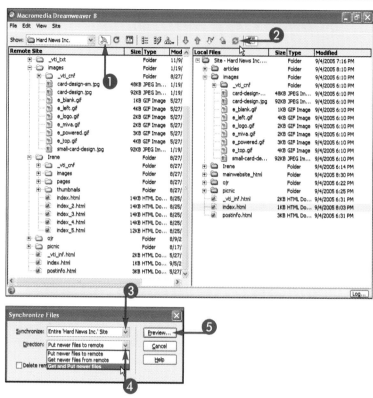

The Synchronize Files dialog box appears.

③ Click here and select the files that you want to synchronize.

④ Click here and select a direction in which you want to copy the files.

You can place the newest copies on both the remote and local sites by selecting **Get and Put newer files**.

⑤ Click **Preview**.

Dreamweaver compares the sites and then lists the files for transfer based on your selections in Steps **3** to **4**.

6 Click to select the files that you do not want to transfer.

7 With the files selected, click **Trash Can** () to remove them from the transfer list.

8 Click **OK**.

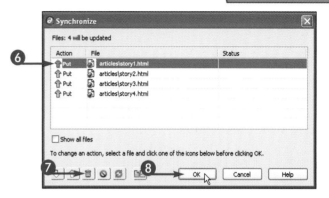

● Dreamweaver transfers the files, and the Synchronize dialog box updates.

The local and remote sites are now synchronized.

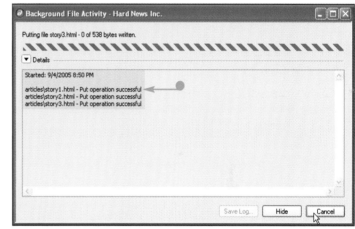

Are there other FTP tools besides those available from Dreamweaver?

Dreamweaver offers the convenience of transferring files without having to open other programs. However, the application uses many system resources and can significantly slow down some computers. There are many good alternatives available. For example, on a PC, you can use WS_FTP. On a Macintosh, you can use Transmit or Fetch. You can download evaluation copies of these programs from www.download.com. Other alternatives for transferring files through FTP include CuteFTP, LeechFTP, and CoffeeCup Direct FTP.

15

Maintaining a Web Site

Maintaining a Web site and keeping its content fresh can be as much work as creating the site. Dreamweaver's site-maintenance tools make updating faster and easier.

View the Site Map

The Site Map view enables you to view your site as a flowchart with lines representing links that connect the document icons. This view also helps you to maintain your site by highlighting broken internal links.

The Dreamweaver Site Map feature should not be confused with site maps that often appear on Web sites. This feature is for organizational use, and is not to be published on your Web site.

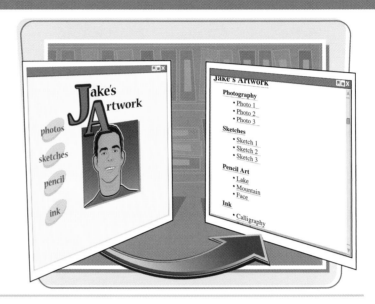

Note: You must first set up a site before you can use the Site Map feature. To set up a site using the Files window, see Chapter 2.

1 In the Files panel, click ⊡.

2 Click **Map view**.

A site map appears in the Files panel. By default, the site map displays the site structure two levels deep, beginning from the home page.

3 In the Files panel, click **Expand Site Panel** (⊡) to expand the map display.

● You can also click and drag the side of the Files panel to expand it.

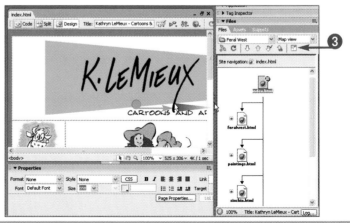

The site map fills the screen.

④ Click .

⑤ Click **Map and Files**.

● The Local Files panel displays on the right side of the screen.

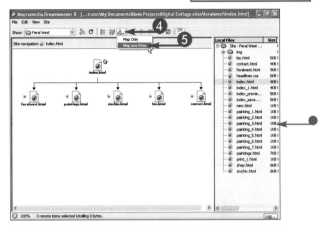

● To view files below the second level, you can click 田.

● External links are marked with an External Link icon (🔲).

To save the site map as a BMP image that you can print or view in an image editor, click **File** and then click **Save Site Map**.

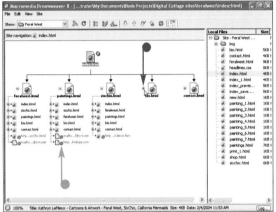

TIPS

How do I fix a broken link in the site map?

A broken chain icon in the site map means that the link to a page is broken. You can fix a broken link by right-clicking (Option + clicking) the destination page and then clicking **Change Link** from the menu that appears. Links can break because a destination page is renamed or deleted.

How can I make changes to the layout of the site map?

From the site window, click **View** and then click **Layout**. The Site Definition window appears, displaying the Site Map Layout options. You can select the home page, specify the number of columns and rows to display, specify whether to identify files by their names or titles, and choose whether to view hidden and dependent files.

Manage
Site Assets

You can view and manage
important elements that appear
in the pages of your site with
the Assets panel.

① Click **Window**.

② Click **Assets**.

● You can also click the **Assets** tab in the Files panel
to open the Assets panel.

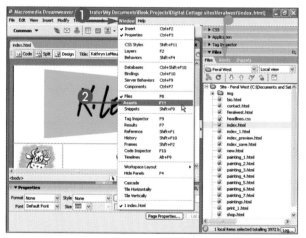

The Assets panel appears, displaying objects from
the selected category.

③ Click the name of any asset to preview it in the
Assets panel.

④ Click and drag the side of the Assets panel to
expand it.

The Assets panel displays in the new dimensions, and previews your selected asset.

⑤ Click a column heading.

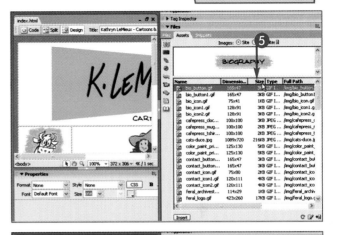

● The assets are now sorted under the selected column heading in descending order. You can click the column again to sort in ascending order.

To view other assets, click a different category button.

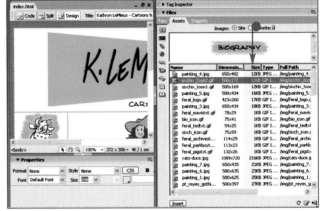

TIP

How are assets organized?

Items in the Assets panel are organized into the following categories:

🖼	**Images**	GIF, JPG, and PNG images
▦	**Color**	Text, background, link, and style-sheet colors
🔖	**URLs**	Accessible external Web addresses
⊘	**Flash**	Flash-based multimedia
▥	**Shockwave**	Shockwave-based multimedia
▣	**Movie**	QuickTime and MPEG movies
◈	**Scripts**	External JavaScript or VBScript files
▤	**Templates**	Page-layout templates
📖	**Library**	Library of reusable page elements

Add Content with the Assets Panel

You can add frequently used content to your site directly from the Assets panel. This technique can be more efficient than using a menu command or the Insert panel.

Add Content with the Assets Panel

INSERT AN IMAGE OR FILE

① Click inside the Document window where you want to insert the asset.

② Click the **Assets** tab to open the Assets panel.

③ Click a category.

④ Click an asset.

⑤ Click **Insert**.

● Dreamweaver inserts the asset into your Document window.

You can also drag and drop the asset from the Assets panel to the Document window.

262

EDIT CONTENT USING THE ASSETS PANEL

1 Click the object to which you want to apply the asset in the Document window.

2 Click a category.

This example uses Colors ().

3 Click an asset.

4 Click **Apply**.

You can also drag and drop the asset from the Assets panel onto the selected object in the Document window.

● Dreamweaver applies the asset in the Document window.

In this example, color is applied to the text.

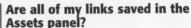

TIPS

How do I copy assets from one site to another?

Click one or more items in the Assets panel, and then right-click (Option + click) the selected assets. From the menu that appears, click **Copy to Site** and then click a site to which you want to copy the assets. The assets appear in the Favorites list under the same category in the other site.

Are all of my links saved in the Assets panel?

Only links to external Web sites and e-mail addresses are saved in the Assets panel. Links to internal pages in your site are not saved in the Assets panel. You can use the link Assets to quickly create new links to Web sites and e-mail addresses to which you have already linked in your site.

Specify Favorite Assets

To make your asset lists more manageable, you can organize assets that you use often into a Favorites list inside each asset category.

① Click the **Assets** tab to open the Assets panel.

② Click a category.

③ Click an asset.

④ Right-click (Option + click) the selected asset and click **Add to Favorites** from the menu that appears.

● You can also click 🔳.

Dreamweaver adds the asset to the category Favorites list.

⑤ Click the **Favorite** option (◯ changes to ◉).

● The selected asset appears in the Favorites category.

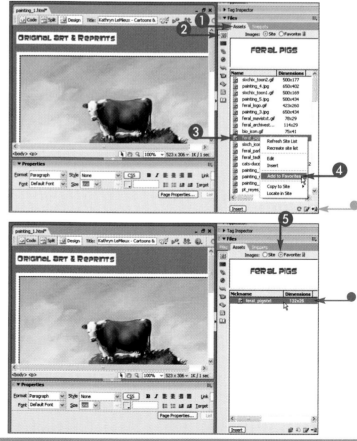

NICKNAME A FAVORITE ASSET

①	Click a category.

②	Click the **Favorite** option (○ changes to ◉).

	You cannot nickname regular assets.

③	Right-click (`Option` + click) an asset.

④	Click **Edit Nickname** from the menu that appears.

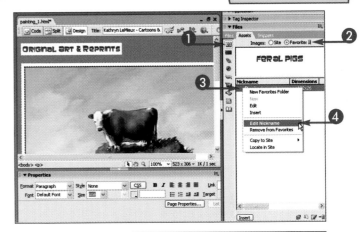

⑤	Type a nickname.

⑥	Press `Enter` (`Return`).

	The nickname appears in the Favorites list.

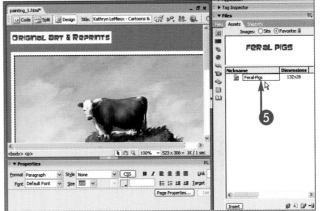

TIPS

How do I remove an item entirely from the Assets panel?

You need to delete the item from your local site folder. You can right-click (`Option` + click) the item in the Files panel, then click **Edit**, and then click **Delete** from the menu that appears. When you return to the Assets panel and click the **Refresh** button (🔁), the asset is gone. You can also delete an item from the Site panel by clicking 🖼 in the Files panel and then following the same steps described above.

How do I add items to the Assets panel?

You do not need to add items. One of the handiest things about the Assets panel is that every time you add an image, external link, e-mail link, color, or multimedia asset to your Web site, Dreamweaver automatically stores it in the Assets panel.

Check a Page In or Out

Dreamweaver provides a Check In/Check Out system that keeps track of files when a team is working on a Web site. For example, when one person checks out a page from the Web server, others cannot access the same file.

When the Check In/Check Out system is off, multiple people can edit the same file at once.

Check a Page In or Out

ENABLE CHECK IN/CHECK OUT

Note: You first need to specify the remote settings, and connect to your remote Web server to use the Check In/Out function. To set up a remote site and to connect to it, see Chapter 14.

1 Click **Site**.

2 Click **Manage Sites**.

The Manage Sites dialog box appears.

3 Click to select the name of a site.

4 Click **Edit**.

The Site Definition dialog box appears.

5 Click the **Advanced** tab.

6 Click **Remote Info**.

7 Click the **Enable file check in and check out** option (changes to ✓).

8 Type your name and e-mail address.

9 Click **OK** to accept your changes.

10 Click **Done** in the Manage Sites dialog box.

Check In/Check Out is now enabled.

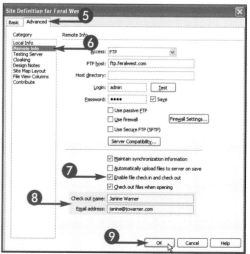

CHECK OUT A FILE

1. Click to select a file in the Files panel that is not checked out, and then right-click (Option + click) it.

2. Click **Check Out**.

   Dreamweaver marks the page as checked out.

CHECK IN A FILE

1. Click to select a file that you have checked out, and then right-click (Option + click) it.

2. Click **Check In**.

   Dreamweaver marks the page as checked in.

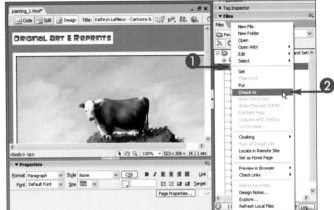

 TIPS

How is a file marked as checked out?

When you check out a file, Dreamweaver creates a temporary LCK file that is stored in the remote site folder while the page is checked out. The file contains information about who has checked the file out. Dreamweaver does not display the LCK files in the file list, but you can see them if you access your remote site with a different FTP program.

Can I e-mail someone who has a file checked out to tell them that I need it?

Yes. Dreamweaver collects usernames and e-mail addresses in the Check In and Check Out fields to make it easy for multiple people who are working on the same Web site to stay in touch. If someone else has a file checked out, you can use the Check In/Out feature to send him or her an e-mail message.

Make Design Notes

If you are working on a site collaboratively, Design Notes enables you to add information about the development status of a file. For example, you can attach information to your Web pages, such as editing history and an author name.

① Open the Web page to which you want to attach a Design Note.

② Click **File**.

③ Click **Design Notes**.

The Design Notes dialog box appears.

④ Click here and select a status for the page.

⑤ Type a note.

⑥ Click **Date** (📅) to enter the current date in the Notes field.

● You can click the **Show when file is opened** option (☐ changes to ☑) to automatically show Design Notes when a file opens.

⑦ Click the **All info** tab.

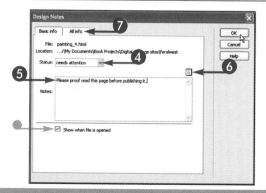

The All info tab displays.

⑧ To enter new information into Design Notes, click ⊞.

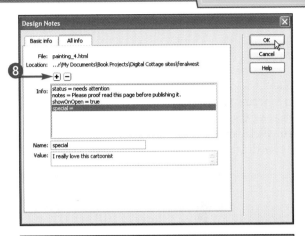

⑨ Type a name and associated value.

● The added value pair appears in the Info section.

You can delete information by clicking it in the Info section and then clicking ⊟.

⑩ Click **OK**.

Dreamweaver makes the Design Note.

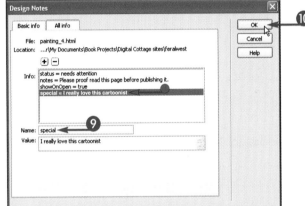

TIPS

How can I view Design Notes?
You can view Design Notes in two ways. First, files with a Design Note have a yellow bubble in the site window. Double-click it to open the Design Note. Alternatively, you can open any file with an attached Design Note, then click **File**, and then click **Design Notes** to open the Design Note.

Are Design Notes private?
Although Design Notes are not linked to the page or displayed in a Web browser, anyone with access to your server can view your Design Notes. If someone is especially clever and your server does not protect the notes folder, then they may find it, even without password access to your site. Ultimately, Design Notes are useful for communication among Web designers, but they are not meant to protect important secrets.

Run a Site Report

Running a site report can help you pinpoint problems in your site, including redundant HTML code in your pages and missing descriptive information such as image `alt` text and page titles. It is a good idea to test your site by running a report before you upload it to a Web server.

Run a Site Report

① Click **Site**.

② Click **Reports** to open the Reports dialog box.

③ Click here and select to run a report on either the entire site or selected files.

④ Click the reports that you want to run (☐ changes to ☑).

⑤ Click **Run**.

Dreamweaver creates a report and displays it in the Results panel.

⑥ Click any tab across the top of the Results panel to display the report.

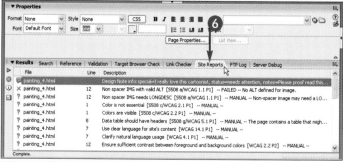

Change a Link Sitewide

You can search and replace all of the hyperlinks on your site that point to a specific address. This is helpful when a page is renamed or deleted and the links to it need to be updated.

Change a Link Sitewide

① Click **Site**.

② Click **Change Link Sitewide**.

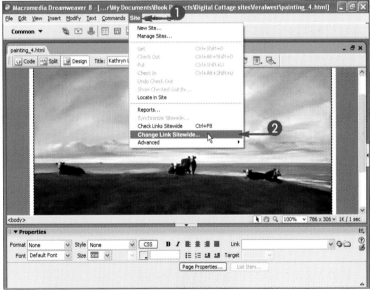

The Change Link Sitewide dialog box appears.

③ Type the old hyperlink destination that you want to change.

④ Type the new hyperlink destination.

The hyperlinks must start with a forward slash (/), and be a mailto: (e-mail) link, or a full URL.

⑤ Click **OK**.

Dreamweaver finds and replaces all instances of the old destination. A dialog box asks you to confirm the changes.

Find and Replace Text

The Find and Replace feature is a powerful tool for making changes to text elements that repeat across many pages. You can find and replace text on your Web page, your source code, or specific HTML tags in your pages.

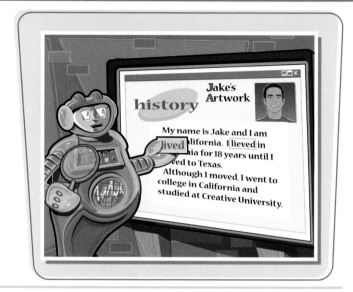

1 Click **Edit**.

2 Click **Find and Replace**.

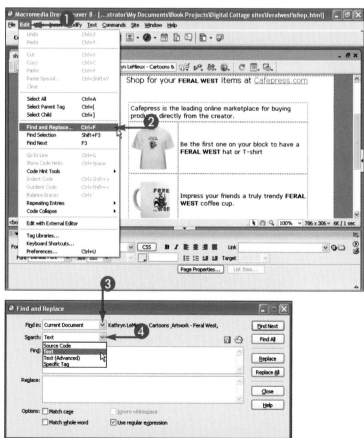

The Find and Replace dialog box appears.

3 Click here and select whether you want to search the entire site or only selected files.

4 Click here and select the type of text that you want to search.

For example, you can select **Text (Advanced)** to find text that is inside a specific tag.

⑤ Type the text that you want to search for in the Find field.

● When searching, you can click **Find Next** to find instances of your query one at a time.

⑥ Type the replacement text in the Replace field.

⑦ Click **Replace** to replace the text instances one at a time.

● You can also click **Replace All** to automatically replace all instances of your text search.

A dialog box may appear asking whether you want to replace text in documents that are not open. Click **Yes**.

● Dreamweaver replaces the text, and the details appear in the bottom of the Find and Replace dialog box.

Can I use the Find and Replace feature to alter HTML code?

Yes. Searching for a string of code is a timesaving way to make changes to a Web site. For example, if you want to alter the body color for every page, then you can search for the HTML body tag and replace it with a different color tag.

Can I use the Find and Replace feature to alter an HTML attribute?

Yes. You can replace attributes to achieve many things. For example, you can change the alignment of the contents of a table (change `align="center"` to `align="right"` in `<td>` tags), change the color of specific text in your page (change `color="green"` to `color="red"` in `<font>` tags), or change the page background color across your site (change `bgcolor="black"` to `bgcolor="white"` in `<body>` tags).

16

Building a Database-Driven Web Site

DYNAMO
A Database
Driven Web Site.

If you are an advanced Dreamweaver user who understands databases, then you can read this chapter to learn how to use server behaviors to create powerful and dynamic Web sites.

The Power of Dynamic Web Sites

Dynamic Web sites use a database to store all kinds of information, and then make the data accessible in various ways. The Web sites that you visit for news, weather, e-mail, forums, and shopping are all examples of dynamic Web technologies.

Database-Driven Web Sites

Dynamic Web pages communicate with a database to display and store content on demand. You can store thousands of pages of information and images in a database. You can then create a handful of dynamic Web pages that allow you to browse or search that content. This is much more efficient than creating a thousand individual HTML pages!

Growth and Maintenance Friendly

Dynamic Web sites are built to handle ever-changing content. For example, e-commerce sites typically consist of a few carefully designed templates that are used to display the contents of the database. Storing data in a database can make it easier to update because when the same data appears on multiple pages in your Web site, you only need to update it once in the database. A database is also more adaptable — you can sort, find, delete, and add information faster in a database than by manually browsing through individual Web pages.

Involve Your Users

Databases are not just about storing content; they can also collect and share data on demand. Web sites like eBay, Yahoo!, and Amazon.com are powered by complex databases. Dynamic Web sites like these enable you to display and receive information from anyone who participates in dynamic areas of the sites. For example, the ability to store user information in a database enables Amazon.com to recommend books based on your previous purchases.

Install a Testing Server

A *Testing Server*, also called an *Application Server*, is software that enables a computer to receive connections from Web browsers. This software supports technologies such as ASP, PHP, and ColdFusion, which act as the liaison between your database and your Web pages.

This section assumes that you are running Windows XP Professional. You may need your Windows XP installation disk to install IIS. If IIS is not available for your version of Windows, then you can download Personal Web Server from www.microsoft.com.

Install a Testing Server

① Click **Start**.

② Click **Control Panel** to open the Control Panel.

③ Click **Add or Remove Programs**.

The Add or Remove Programs dialog box appears.

④ Click **Add/Remove Windows Components**.

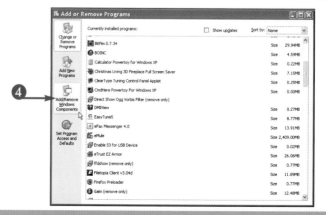

The Windows Components Wizard window appears.

⑤ Click **Internet Information Services (IIS)**
(☐ changes to ☑).

If Internet Information Services (IIS) is already
checked, click **Cancel** and skip to Step **15**.

⑥ Click **Next**.

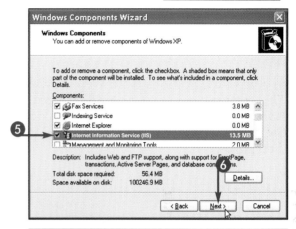

A progress screen lets you know how the installation
is going.

Note: *You may receive a prompt asking you to insert your Windows
Installation CD-ROM into the CD-ROM drive. If you receive this prompt,
then complete this step.*

The Windows Component Wizard completion page
appears.

⑦ Click **Finish**.

Why does Windows need the installation CD-ROM?
Windows is made up of thousands of individual files
and programs. In order to save space on your
computer's hard drive, Windows copies only
the files that it needs when you originally
install it. When you install a Windows
component, such as Internet Information
Services, Windows sometimes needs to
copy these files from the CD-ROM and
put them on your computer's hard drive.

continued

Windows XP Professional ships with Internet Information Server (IIS). IIS is an application server that processes Active Server Pages (ASP) and makes it easy for you to create dynamic pages.

Install a Testing Server *(continued)*

⑧ Click **Start**.

⑨ Click **All Programs**.

⑩ Click **Administrative Tools**.

⑪ Click **Internet Information Services**.

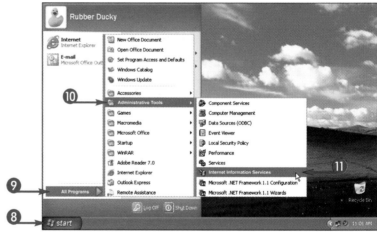

The Internet Information Services window appears.

⑫ Right-click **Default Web Site** (🖳).

⑬ Click **Properties**.

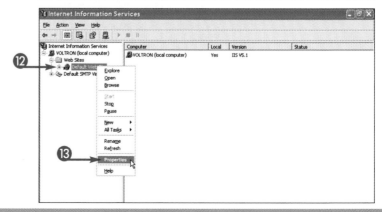

The Default Web Site Properties dialog box appears.

Note: *IIS allows you to control various Web site settings, such as public folder browsing. For more information on IIS, visit www.microsoft.com.*

⑭ Click **OK** to close the window.

⑮ Open your Web browser.

⑯ Type **http://localhost/**.

The default Testing Server page displays, telling you that the server was installed correctly.

● This page also tells you where to move your Web site. The path is usually at c:\inetpub\wwwroot\.

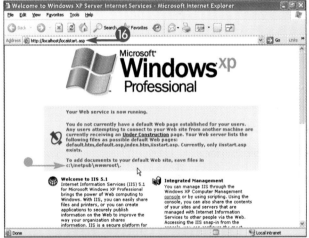

TIP

What should I do if I cannot find the Administrative Tools folder?

Windows does not automatically show the Administrative Tools folder. To show the folder:

① Right-click **Start**.

② Click **Properties**.

③ Click **Customize**.

④ Click the **Advanced** tab.

⑤ Click the **Display on the All Programs menu** option (○ changes to ◉).

⑥ Click **OK**.

⑦ Click **OK**.

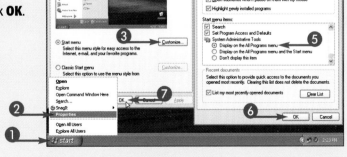

Create a Database Connection

A data source name, or DSN, is used to store database connection settings. Acting as a bookmark, it allows you to conveniently connect to your database from applications without defining the settings for the database every time. You must first create a database before defining a DSN.

This example uses a simple database that was created with Microsoft Access 2000, a popular database program for Windows.

Create a Database Connection

① Click **Start**.

② Click **All Programs**.

③ Click **Administrative Tools**.

④ Click **Data Sources (ODBC)**.

Windows XP hides folders that you do not regularly use. Click the double-arrow down to expand hidden items if the Data Sources option is not visible.

The ODBC Data Source Administrator dialog box appears.

⑤ Click the **System DSN** tab.

⑥ Click **Add**.

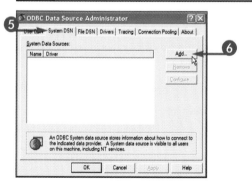

The Create New Data Source dialog box appears with a list of database drivers.

⑦ Click **Microsoft Access Driver**.

⑧ Click **Finish**.

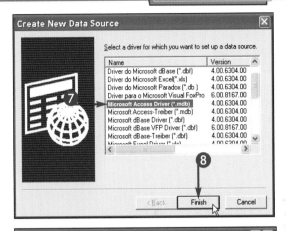

The ODBC Microsoft Access Setup dialog box appears.

⑨ Type a unique, descriptive name for your database.

⑩ Click **Select**.

continued

TIPS

What is a server-side programming language? Is HTML a server-side programming language?

HTML is a *markup* language, meaning that its primary use is to display content. However, it was developed to connect with other technologies. Server-side programming languages such as ASP, PHP, JSP, and ColdFusion are languages that are used to create programs that reside on a server and make database communication possible. Dreamweaver 8 server behaviors write server-side programming code for you.

What is the difference between a system DSN, a user DSN, and a file DSN?

All three DSN types store the same kind of database connectivity information. You use a system DSN when you want every user on the computer to have access to the database. A user DSN only allows specific computer users to access the database, usually the user who creates it. Both system and user DSNs store the information inside the Registry. A file DSN creates a DSN file, storing the information inside this text file instead of the registry.

If your application server is running on a Windows system, then you can use a DSN to connect your dynamic Web pages to a database.

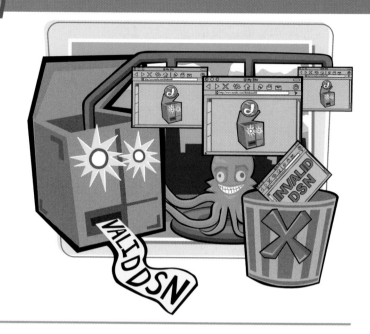

Create a Database Connection *(continued)*

The Select Database dialog box appears.

⑪ Click here and select the drive where the database is located.

⑫ Click the folder in which the database is located.

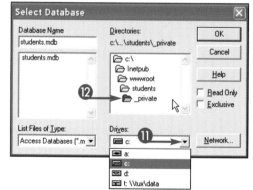

⑬ Click the desired MDB file (Microsoft Access Database File).

⑭ Click **OK**.

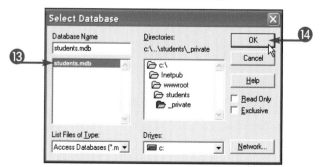

● The path of the database file appears in the ODBC Microsoft Access Setup dialog box.

⓯ Click **OK** to close the ODBC Microsoft Access Setup dialog box.

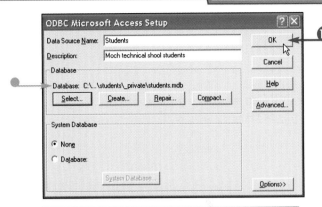

● Windows creates the database connection, and lists it in the ODBC Data Source Administrator dialog box.

⓰ Click **OK** to close the ODBC Data Source Administrator dialog box.

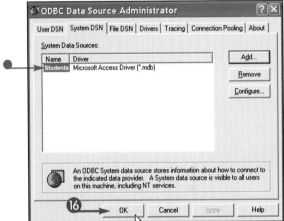

TIP

How can I connect to a database without creating a DSN?

① Click **Window**.

② Click **Database**.

③ In the Database panel, click ➕ on the Databases panel.

④ Click **Custom Connection String**.

⑤ In the Custom Connection String dialog box, type a name for the connection.

⑥ Type a string for the connection.

For example, to connect to students.mdb, located in the c:\data\ folder, type **driver=[Microsoft Access Driver (*.mdb)];dbq=c:\data\students.mdb;** as the connection string.

⑦ Click **OK**.

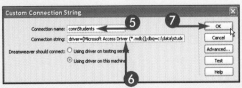

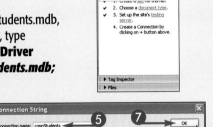

Configure a Dynamic Web Site

Dynamic Web pages do not display database content when you open them directly from a Web browser. As a result, you must configure Dreamweaver to use your testing server. These features create a seamless authoring environment for you.

Configure a Dynamic Web Site

ASSOCIATE THE TESTING SERVER

① Click **Site**.

② Click **Manage Sites**.

The Manage Sites dialog box appears.

③ Click a site.

④ Click **Edit**.

Note: You must either move all of the contents of your site into your testing server area (usually a folder inside c:\inetpub\wwwroot), or configure IIS to point to its current folder. For more information about the testing server, see the section "Install a Testing Server."

The Site Definition dialog box appears.

⑤ Click the **Advanced** tab.

⑥ Click **Testing Server**.

⑦ Click here and select **ASP VBScript**.

⑧ Click here and select **Local/Network**.

⑨ Click here and select where your site is located on your computer.

⑩ Type the path to your local site folder, starting with the URL prefix **http://localhost/**.

⑪ Click **OK**.

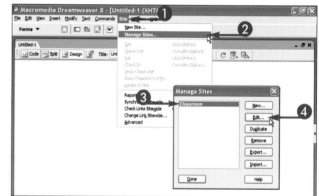

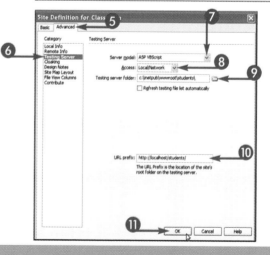

ASSOCIATE AND TEST YOUR CONNECTION

① Click the **Application** panel ▼ to see the checklist of items that are necessary to test your connection.

② Click any unchecked links.

If the Testing Server option is not checked, then you must verify that one is associated with your site, and ensure that IIS is running properly.

③ Click ➕ and select **Data Source Name (DSN)**.

The Data Source Name (DSN) dialog box appears.

④ Type a connection name.

⑤ Click here and select your DSN.

● To create, edit, or troubleshoot your connections, click **Define**.

⑥ Click **Test**.

A dialog box appears, confirming your connection.

⑦ Click **OK**.

A yellow cylinder appears in your database panel, representing a working connection.

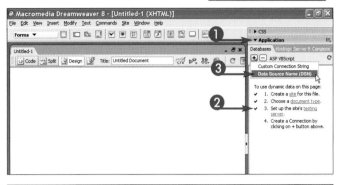

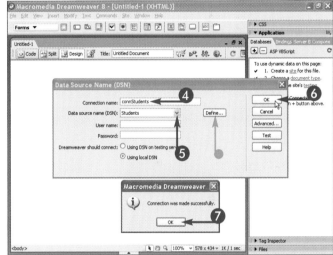

Can I open dynamic Web pages directly through my browser instead of installing a testing server?

No. Web browsers are not capable of understanding server-side programming languages. Instead of displaying a dynamic Web page, the Web browser displays the programming code that comprises the page. Think of the testing server as a person who translates the results of this code into HTML, a language that your Web browser understands.

Create a Recordset

A *recordset* is a virtual group of items of which you can request retrieval from a database. You can then manipulate and display this selection of data on the Web page. A recordset can contain one or more fields, such as the name, address, or phone number fields in a contact database.

Requested: **Zombies**
Retrieved: **Zombies**
(1965) Undead Records.

FINDING RECORDSET

Create a Recordset

① Click **File**.

② Click **New** to open a new document.

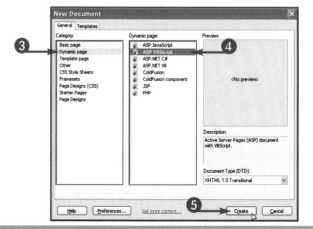

A New Document dialog box appears.

③ Click **Dynamic page**.

④ Click **ASP VBScript**.

⑤ Click **Create**.

An untitled page appears.

⑥ Click the **Bindings** tab.

⑦ Click +

⑧ Click **Recordset (Query)**.

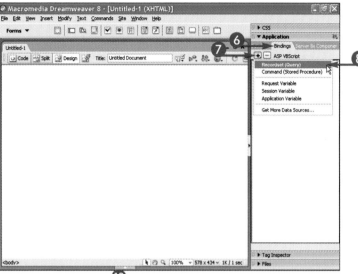

The Recordset dialog box appears.

⑨ Type a name for your recordset.

⑩ Click ▾.

⑪ Click a connection.

Note: *Your connection is the DSN that you assigned to this site. For information about configuring a dynamic Web site, see the section "Configure a Dynamic Web Site."*

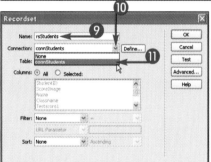

Does it matter if I choose ASP VBScript or ASP JavaScript for new dynamic Web pages?

No, it does not make a difference. Dreamweaver inserts code, either JavaScript or VBScript, to create your dynamic Web pages. The only time that it makes a difference is if you want to make changes to the code that Dreamweaver inserts. If this is the case, then you should choose the scripting language with which you are more familiar. For more information about scripting in ASP pages, visit www.microsoft.com/scripting/ or www.4guysfromrolla.com/.

continued

A *recordset* serves as a temporary
mediator between the databases
where the information is stored
and the dynamic Web page
application.

Create a Recordset *(continued)*

⑫ Click ⊡.

⑬ Click the table that you want to use to create a
recordset.

⑭ Click **Test** to view the recordset that you have
created.

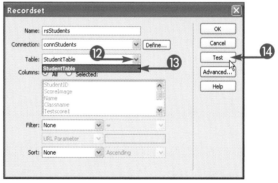

The Test SQL Statement dialog box appears.

⑮ Click **OK** to close the test screen.

Filtering and sorting are optional. If you choose not
to set either menu, then your recordset displays
everything in the table as it appears in the database.

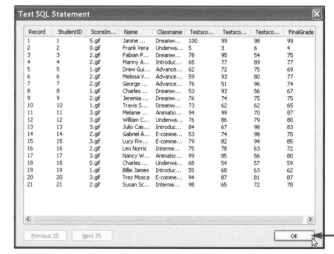

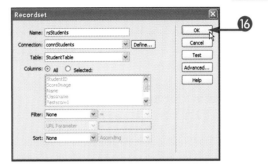

16 Click **OK** to close the Recordset dialog box.

Dreamweaver creates a recordset within your Bindings panel.

● You can click ⊞ to expand the column names of your recordset.

● Lightning bolts (⚡) represent the table columns in your recordset.

● To modify a recordset, double-click its name from the Bindings panel.

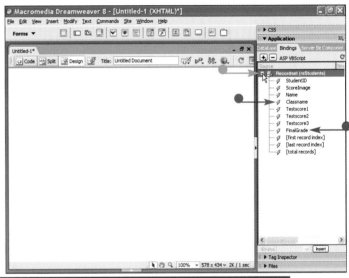

TIP

How do I organize database content on a Web page?

1 Create a recordset by following Steps **1** to **13** in this section.

2 In the Recordset dialog box, click the **Sort** ▾ and select the field by which you want to sort.

3 Click here and select the condition by which you want to sort, for example, **Ascending** or **Descending**.

4 Click **Test** to preview the sorted results in the Test Query SQL Statement dialog box.

5 Click **OK**.

6 Click **OK** to save your sorted recordset.

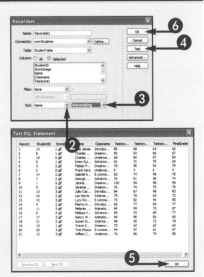

Add a Record

Instead of entering information into your database with desktop software, you can create your own Web page forms that enable you to input content into your database using a Web browser.

① Create a recordset containing the tables to which you want to add a record.

Note: For more information, see the section "Create a Recordset."

② Click where you want to insert the form.

③ Click **Insert**.

④ Click **Application Objects**.

⑤ Click **Insert Record**.

⑥ Click **Record Insertion Form Wizard**.

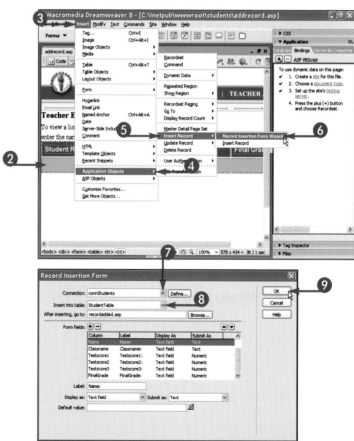

The Record Insertion Form dialog box appears.

⑦ Click here and select your connection.

⑧ Click here and select your table.

⑨ Click **OK**.

A completed form appears with highlighted fields and assigned server behaviors.

You can open your Web browser and test the page in your testing server.

Similar to the Record Insertion Form object, this server object creates a form that allows you to view content from a database in form fields, modify them on the page, and submit your changes back to the database.

Update a Record

① Create a recordset containing the tables to which you want to add a record.

Note: *For more information, see the section "Create a Recordset."*

② Click where you want to insert the form.

③ Click **Insert**.

④ Click **Application Objects**.

⑤ Click **Update Record**.

⑥ Click **Record Update Form Wizard**.

The Record Update Form dialog box appears.

⑦ Click here and select a connection.

⑧ Click here and select your table.

⑨ Click here and select a unique key for the table.

⑩ Click **OK**.

A highlighted form and Submit button appear.

You can open your Web browser and test the page in your testing server.

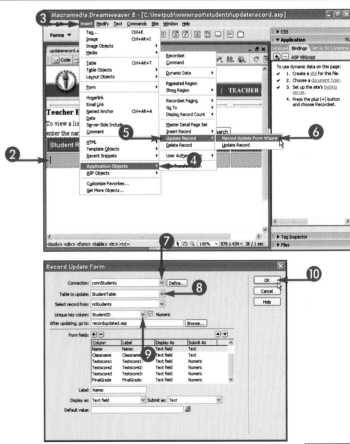

Add Recordset Paging

You can use the server behavior Recordset Paging to display the amount of information that you want on each page. This is useful because most search engines limit their pages to 20 results per page. You can use dynamic links or buttons to navigate to the rest of the content.

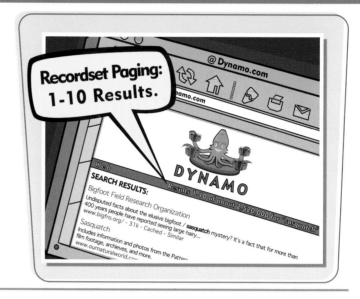

Add Recordset Paging

REPEAT A REGION

1 Select the regions of the page that you want to repeat.

Note: The region that you select must contain items from your recordset.

2 Click the **Server Behaviors** tab.

3 Click ➕

4 Click **Repeat Region**.

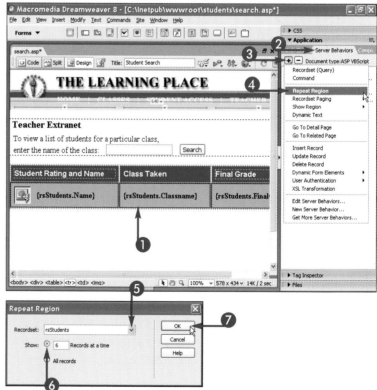

The Repeat Region dialog box appears.

5 Click here and select the recordset that contains the data that you want to repeat.

6 Click the **Show** option and then type the number of records you want to appear on a page (◯ changes to ◉).

7 Click **OK**.

PAGINATE YOUR DYNAMIC PAGE

A Repeat tab appears around the region that you specified.

⑧ Click the **Server Behaviors** tab.

⑨ Click ⊞.

⑩ Click **Recordset Paging**.

⑪ Click a paging behavior from the menu.

The most commonly used paging behaviors are to move to either the next or the previous record.

A highlighted text link appears on your page.

⑫ Preview the page in a Web browser.

⑬ Click the new links to browse your database.

The Show Region enables you to automatically hide navigational links. Click the **Next** button or link, then click **Show Region** from the Server Behaviors panel, and then click **Show If Not Last Record** to control the display of navigation options.

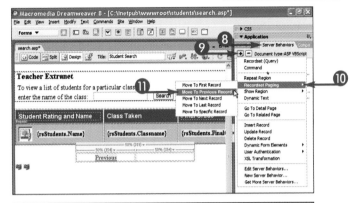

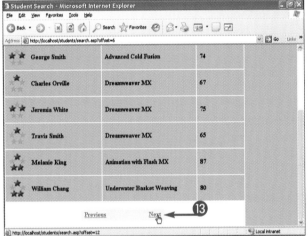

 TIP

How can I protect my dynamic forms from hackers?

First, save all the data-entry screens in an obscurely named area of your Web site. Next, use simple password authentication. IIS allows you to modify the properties of a folder to activate directory security. Finally, install an SSL certificate so that passwords that are sent to unlock this directory cannot be intercepted. To purchase a certificate and to learn more about SSL, visit www.thawte.com and www.verisign.com.

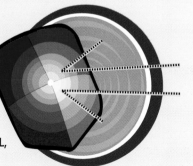

Create a Site Search

You can create a *site search* to quickly and easily enable Web site visitors to locate records in a database. Creating a site search essentially combines several sections of this chapter. You must create the search form, define the search parameters in a recordset, and then designate where the search results appear with the Repeated Region server behavior.

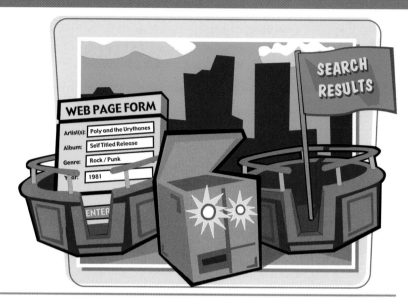

Create a Site Search

① Create a new dynamic page using ASP JavaScript technology.

Note: For more information about creating a recordset, see the section "Create a Recordset."

② Create a form with a text field and a Submit button.

The form method should be post by default.

Note: To create a form, see Chapter 11.

③ Type a name for your text field.

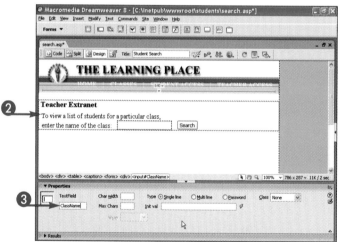

④ Click [+].

⑤ Click **Recordset (Query)** to open the Recordset dialog box.

⑥ Click here and select the connection and table for your site search.

⑦ Click here and select the column in the database that matches the field with which you want to search.

⑧ Click here and select how the filter should behave.

You can select **contains** for flexible searching, and select **=** for exact matches.

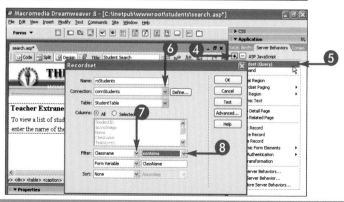

9 Click here and select **Form Variable** as your filter style.

10 Type the name of your text field as the filter style variable, using the name of the field that you created in Step **3**.

11 Click **Test** to open the Test Value dialog box.

12 Type a search term that is in the specified area of your database.

13 Click **OK**.

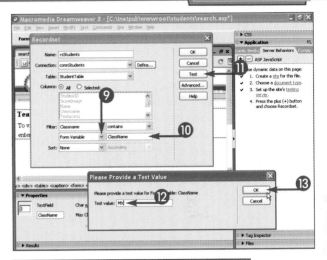

The Test SQL Statement dialog box displays the filtered results. In this example, the test value was the word MX.

14 Click **OK** to close the Test SQL dialog box.

15 Click **OK** in the Recordset dialog box to save your filtered recordset.

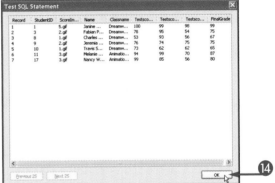

 TIP

How do I create a site search that indexes the Web pages of my site like a search engine?

Dreamweaver 8 does not offer any page-indexing features. However, there are third-party extensions that you can install, as well as manual indexing methods. Visit http://exchange.macromedia.com and search on the term *search*. Atomz Search and Deva Tools are among the best third-party indexing extensions. To create your own index, add a table in your database that contains URLs and keywords about your pages, and then create a site search that looks at those keywords. Your repeated region can then display the URLs to those relevant pages in your database, just as a search engine does.

continued

A Web site user can conduct a site search by formulating a recordset with a dynamic value set. The form allows the user to input what the recordset filters. The user then submits the form, the server behaviors perform the filter script, and the filtered data is returned as a recordset that displays on the Web page.

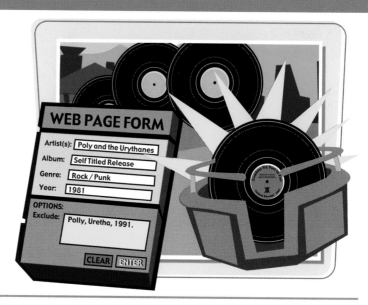

Create a Site Search *(continued)*

⑯ Create a table with the fields from the recordset that you want to display as search results.

⑰ Apply the Repeat Region server behavior to your table.

Note: *For information on repeating a region, see the section "Add a Recordset Paging."*

The Repeat Region dialog box appears.

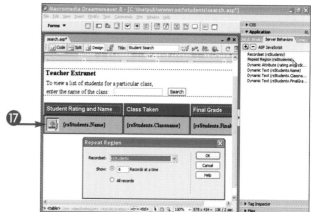

⑱ Select your repeat region table.

⑲ Click the **Server Behaviors** tab.

⑳ Click ➕.

㉑ Click **Show Region**.

㉒ Click **Show Region If Recordset Is Not Empty**.

A dialog box appears.

㉓ To confirm your recordset, click here and select it from the drop-down menu.

㉔ Click **OK**.

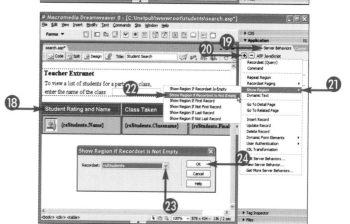

㉕ Preview this page in your Web browser.

㉖ Type a search value in your form.

㉗ Click **Search**.

● The search results appear below.

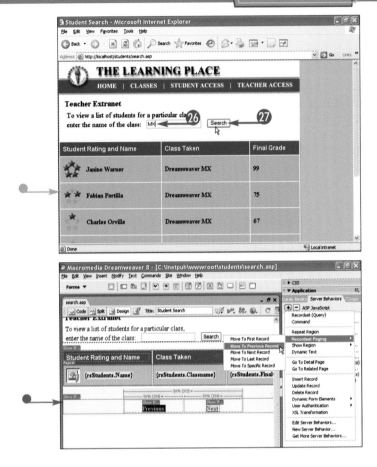

Note: *To apply the Recordset Paging server behavior to help you to navigate through a long list of search results, see the section "Add a Recordset Paging."*

● Remember to apply the appropriate Show Region behaviors to your Next and Previous links. Otherwise, both of these links appear before you perform a search.

TIP

Where can I learn more about creating dynamic Web sites?

Dynamic Web sites are highly complex and most people who do site development are highly trained, experienced programmers. This chapter is designed just to introduce you to Dreamweaver's database features. If you want to learn more, visit www.macromedia.com and check out the Developer's section for more information. If you are an Apple user, visit www.mamp.info for more on dynamic site creation.

Index

Index

Index